About the Author

Marvin Kistler wrote *The Stranger Within*, published in 1995, about the two halves of the brain and how they function and relate to everyday life. In 2008, he wrote *The War Between the Ego and You; The Internal Battles for Control of the Self.*

He has a B.S. degree in Education from Miami University in Oxford, Ohio; a B.S. degree in electrical engineering from South Florida University; one year of graduate school at the University of Mississippi in psychology and a Silver Life Master at duplicate bridge. He also dabbles in stand-up comedy at a local comedy club.

Marvin Kistler

EMOTIONAL FREEDOM WITH NO FEAR, NO ANGER, AND NO INSECURITY

AUSTIN MACAULEY PUBLISHERS™

LONDON • CAMBRIDGE • NEW YORK • SHARJAH

Ordering Information:
Quantity sales: special discounts are available on quantity purchases by corporations, associations, and others. For details, contact the publisher at the address below.

Publisher's Cataloging-in-Publication data
Kistler, Marvin
Emotional Freedom with No Fear, No Anger, and No Insecurity

ISBN 9781641827492 (Paperback)
ISBN 9781641827508 (Hardback)
ISBN 9781645364702 (ePub e-book)

Library of Congress Control Number: 2019907934

www.austinmacauley.com/us

First Published (2020)
Austin Macauley Publishers LLC
40 Wall Street, 28th Floor
New York, NY 10005
USA

mail-usa@austinmacauley.com
+1 (646) 5125767

Part One

Chapter 1

We are not instinctual creatures. We develop and learn from each other. To discover solutions to troubling problems, you need to have help, whether from parents, friends, books, etc. You need to learn the social and behavioral tools and skills that can assist you in coping with life's daily challenges.

Emotional freedom allows you to handle any situation. It will let you feel comfortable under any condition. It will provide you with self-confidence that will empower you to take care of problematic circumstances. Emotional freedom will allow you to realize your full emotional growth as a complete, mature human being. When you become emotionally free, you'll develop a disposition and character of merit that will transform you into someone whom others will find interesting, provocative, and inspiring.

We may be advanced technologically, educationally, and intellectually, but our culture functions at a superficial level of social development. "If all men are created equal," then emotional freedom has the potential to make this famous saying a possibility. An egalitarian culture can raise the social development of a society to a very high functional level.

It is only with the emotional growth of the individual that we evolve as a group, as a community, or as a society. It will never happen from the top down. It can only happen from the bottom up.

The problem is, we have not had the guidance that would allow us to discover the many layers and the deep complexity of ourselves. And we have not been given the knowledge to enable us to be master of our emotions and, that would make us successful and achieve our intentions.

With help, you can thrive and achieve emotional growth to become a confident person who is free of fear, free of anger, and free of insecurities. Advice is given that will show you how you can be proficient at anything you wish. Copious behavioral skills are described to help you do this and to help you build relationships and friendships.

When troubles arise in a relationship, knowledge is provided to resolve those problems to establish a stable bond. You become an emotionally free person when you use these behavioral skills to achieve a mastery of yourself.

To be a commander of the self is an aspiration you can acquire with knowledge and guidance.

The intention is to guide and explain the skills that will strengthen your character, to allow you to handle stressful conditions. This information will give you the confidence in yourself, so you can become a person who is emotionally free of stressful, emotional drama. You are not truly a free person until you have command of yourself. There is an adage that says, "He that rules the self is greater than he who captures a city." You rule the self when you are free of fear, free of anger, and free of insecurities.

The more significant purpose of this book is to enable you to enhance your character, your rational, creative mind, and your personality to generate connections with others in a supportive environment.

This book should be reread because there will be changes to your approach, attitudes, beliefs, and ideas about what's important in life so that each additional perusal will take on new and more significance understanding and meaning, that you will want to experience and live.

****

The ego wants to control and rule you. It does that by keeping you distraught with undesirable difficulties like guilt, restlessness, boredom, regret, irritability, depression, fear, anger, and insecurity. Only the nuclei and neural pathways located in the limbic brain of the ego can create these negative emotions. (See the following illustration.) You, the conscience self, have no neural networks in your brain to generate these stressful feelings. When the ego's thoughts are in your head, it takes control of your mind. The ego needs control of your brain before these stressful feelings can affect you. These disruptive effects disappear when you block the ego's thoughts with the behavioral tools provided for you to use and practice.

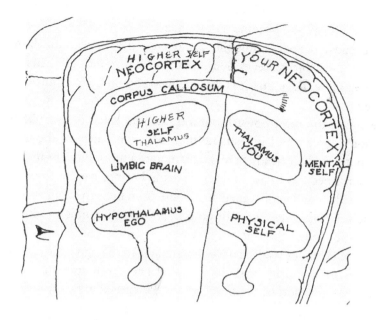

The hippocampus is your memory bank and acts as the neocortex of the ego's limbic brain.[1,2] This separate brain of the ego means that it's an independent entity. It has different beliefs and attitudes that are the very opposite of yours. The ego will manipulate you to fulfill its agenda and desires. Its greatest craving is to control you and to control others.

The ego wants to be the boss who dominates. It can do this as long as it remains incognito and hidden, so we are unaware and ignorant of its abilities and skillfulness to be in charge of us. If we were to try to investigate further to learn about our ego, the egos of many people would become scared, angry, or insecure which they may experience as extreme uneasiness. Any attempt to gain knowledge about their ego will usually result in agitation, stress, and tension to cause them to back away and avoid developing any knowledge about their ego. This routine is how the ego stays in command of our mind to create most of our problems and this way it continues to control of us.

****

The ego has an obsessive-compulsive drive to be thinking all the time. When the ego's thoughts are in your head, it takes over control of your mind with thoughts about the past or the future. Thoughts are important. Thoughts are things that describe who you are. For a thought to come from you, it takes exertion or work on your part. The ego's thoughts come into the head without effort. When the ego is thinking, it takes command of the mind and its agenda and beliefs rule, as you become a bystander.

It is because the ego's thoughts can occupy the mind so much of the time that the ego therefore believes that it is in control of the self. This realization leads the ego to believe that it is the one who should be in control and should be obeyed.

The ego is the most powerful and influential force in everybody's lives. The reason people don't investigate their ego is because of the thoughts the ego will put into their heads to make them avoid the subject of their ego; like, 'Oh we don't need to know this,' or 'This is boring, we are fine the way we are.' These ideas and many others that come from the ego suppress any interest about itself, because the ego will go into an offensive mode to keep us from acquiring knowledge about itself.

Knowledge about itself is very threatening to the ego as it can undermine its position of authority and dominance. The more immature or socially dysfunctional a person is, the more power the ego exerts over him or her and the greater the danger the ego will experience. If that person were to investigate further, the ego would not put up with that behavior for one-second. The ego can have such significant power over this person that it can control his or her behavior. If the person does not obey, he or she will suffer the consequence of considerable fear, anger, and insecurity.

The ego can also interfere or hinder your ability to understand what you read about the ego. It does that by continually intruding with its thoughts to make you keep rereading threatening information about itself. Also, while reading this information, the ego will create feelings of impatience, boredom, or restlessness to influence you to just give up. So, the ego fights hard to keep information about itself away from you.

****

The ego has tricked you into thinking that you, the rational, logical, and conscious self, are in control of your life, while it really believes that it, the ego, is the real leader who controls the self. This duplicity will cease when you gain the knowledge that you are the lord and master of the ego. You are the absolute ruler. The ego is your subject, under your authority, who must obey your directives. The ego must know that you're the boss and must follow your instructions and must give way to following your beliefs and intentions.

The higher self and the 'body' are also subordinates who will follow your directives. The 'body' operates with a lot of inertia, so it is in need of your guidance to help maintain good physical health. Once you've shown the 'body' that you're the ruler of the self and not the ego, then if you get a cramp in your leg, you can tell the 'body' to relax that muscle, and it will do that for you.

The ego can also control the 'body,' who because of the ego's emotional immaturity can cause the 'body' to make you feel poorly or ill. Some egos are not too concerned with an illness, because of the attention it gets, and because an illness causes you to lose energy that will increases the ego's control of your mind. The only way for you to be able to do anything about the stress the ego creates within the 'body,' like tension in the gut is for you to assert your dominance and control over the ego.

****

The ego creates an unhappy life. Life should be wonderful. When information about our inner selves is lacking, then we don't have the insight and the understanding we need to thrive and to develop a magnificent life. The ego needs to be stern because it wants to improve the self. But its seriousness can be so persistent that it promotes a lack of joy in us.

If you have suffered a loss, like a mate, friend, income, or respect, the ego can make you ill or sick by continually recalling memories involved with those events. It's not that the ego is mean-spirited, but it thrives in this type of drama where it can be in control. However, you cannot allow the ego to rule over you and make you unhappy by living in the past. You are meant to rule over the ego and live in the present.

The ego dislikes joyfulness and happiness because it robs it of its authority and interferes with what it wants to do.

A dissatisfaction with life increases the control the ego has over us. The ego gains power from the stress it cultivates.

When the ego gets involved with a social situation, its gravity quickly turns into a desire to control the circumstances or the behaviors of others.

****

The ego cannot control your mind when you are in the present. The ego recalls events from the past and is concerned about what could happen in the future. It relives past experiences or worries about what could occur in the future. It does not like the 'present.'

People hand over the control of their minds to the ego because they are unable to distinguish the difference between the conscious entity known as you from the entirely different entity called the ego. As a result, people fail to separate themselves from this emotionally immature being, called the ego.

11

Because of the lack of knowledge about the ego's existence, people have no idea about the many ways the ego can maneuver and manipulate them. Other names for the ego could be a charlatan, a trickster, a scam artist who can pull the wool over their eyes, and guide us down a path to its garden of beliefs and agendas.

****

We need to work with our ego if our goals are to be achieved. Even though it has no integrity and is unable to love, the ego is our engine of energy which we need. Most have no idea or no understanding of the ego's ability to influence how we think, the emotions we feel, the reason we sometimes act the way we do with others, and the control the ego can wield over us when we are alone. Prisoners placed in solitary confinement can be driven insane by their egos if they don't have any of the behavioral tools that can control their ego. People are provided here with the skills needed to prevent that from happening.

****

Our ego, our judge, is evaluating everything we do and everything we don't do. It judges everything we feel and everything we don't feel. The ego is assessing and judging us all the time. It is judging everyone else also, based on what it believes, and based on its flawed sense of justice and injustice. The ego becomes the prosecutor, the judge, and the jury to find us guilty to justify its desire to sentence us and punish us, so we experience regret, sadness, guilt, shame, embarrassment, or other similar stresses that provide the ego more access to our mind, which increases its control.

When the ego judges others and believes they are guilty, then it brings about feelings of disapproval, dislike, intolerance, and aversion. The ego may judge others negatively, because it's decided they are lazy, dumb, fat, skinny, or too peculiar; it may judge them detrimentally because of the color of their skin, their gender, their sexual preferences, or their political beliefs. These criticisms of others give rise to feelings of hostility and hate in the ego.

The ego may want to avoid feeling of joyfulness and happiness, but it is captivated by feelings of hate. The ego loves the feelings that hate generates. Because the ego enjoys hate so much, then when others with similar sentiments find each other, there develops a contagion, as their hatred reinforces each other to strengthen their mutual beliefs.

Although you and the higher self may believe in love, the ego without any restriction will develop an opposite belief system that loves hate. Hate gives the ego almost total control over you. With hate, the ego belief systems dominate instead of yours; this allows the ego to take control over your rational and creative minds and take command of you. Hate will eventually destroy the hater, emotionally, mentally, psychologically, socially, and physically.

This feeling of excitement that hate generates in the ego often creates a pack, gang or fringe movement that a tyrant can utilize to create a base of fervent followers who will forego a lot of their freedoms and their rational, creative minds for the thrilling drama that the ego's beliefs can generate. Without hatred, contempt, and hostility a dictator can never rule a community, a state, or a nation.

The question is, who will rule, you or the ego. The ultimate commander of the self is a black-or-white issue. There is no gray area here. You are the adult. You are the only rational, logical, intelligent one who can take over the care and the responsibilities to govern and look out for the well-being of the other three entities or selves.

****

Someone who commands the self has no fears, no insecurities, and expresses no anger. Until you understand and learn about your power of control and authority over the ego, you will never be truly free. There is only one type of freedom that you can have control over, and that is emotional freedom. Your own unique freedom is imperative for you to be a ruler of the self.

When you permit the ego to focus on the future, and you allow it to occupy the mind continuously, then the ego can be in almost total control of you. This dominance by the ego can cause you to suffer from an obsessive-compulsive disorder (OCD) or a phobia.

When you yield to the ego and let it occupy your mind continuously, you will probably develop a phobia or OCD, you have allowed the ego to be in charge of you, the conscious, rational self. You have given away the rule of the self. You have let the ego be the boss, instead of you. The ego has become the commander-in-chief over you, and it will tell you what you can do and what you cannot do. If you do not follow the ego's agenda, you will suffer the painful consequences of paralyzing fear, or one of the other many stressful, adverse strategies, such as, an ability to create a panic attack, or by making you feel uncomfortable with constant, obsessive thoughts, or tense with an obsession to repeat some physical act, which it can dole out as long as it has command of your mind.

****

The solution to emotional problems, like fear, anger, and insecurities, may appear to be counterintuitive, but the answer is awareness! It seems like an easy solution that may even sound unbelievable, but constant awareness is not only the hardest achievement you can ever accomplish, but also it is the greatest achievement you can ever accomplish. Awareness gets the ego out of your head and blocks the ego from thinking.

Awareness stops the ego dead in its tracks. Awareness puts up a barrier that prevents the ego from controlling your mind. Without access to your mind, it can no longer create negative, emotional, and mental stressful states of fear, anger, and insecurities.

When the ego is in your head thinking, you are not mindful of what's going on within you or around you. You are unconscious in the sense that the ego has taken over your mind and you have lost the valuable asset of awareness! Awareness is the behavioral tool on which you can take back control of the self and achieve emotional freedom.

****

The ego keeps its concerns and its beliefs in the forefront of our minds to influence every decision we make. The more time we allow the ego to occupy our minds, the more likely the ego's goals and beliefs become our opinion. We've allowed the ego to misguide us and be in charge of us by a neglect of our responsibilities. Even though we would not want this, we have given into this obsessive-compulsive energy of the ego, because there is no source of information available to us to know how to harness and control the power of the ego.

When the ego has control of our mind, we have lost our rational, creative advantage of using our brain's neocortical gray matter. The ego is not rational; it resides in the uneasiness of our simple, unrefined, limbic brain.

The top frontal part of our neocortex is where problem-solving and rational thought occurs. But not realizing the inability of the ego to create logical, rational thoughts, we accept the ego's unjustifiable beliefs as part of our natural self and that influences us to make decisions, make errors in judgment, and make predictions that are wrong.

****

We use rationalization to justify thoughts that lead us to behave inappropriately or without discernment. The result is that we use rationalization as an excuse for allowing the ego to influence us to behave the way we do.

The ego's irrational or unacceptable agenda, motive, and feeling causes people to engage in rationalization as a defense against feeling ridiculous in front of others. When the ego causes people to do something foolish, because of its thoughts, they have to perform a rationalization to give a seemingly good reason, to justify the way they acted and provide an explanation which (though false) could seem tolerable by plausible means.

People are aware of the inconsistent thoughts coming into their head that need to be justified. Since they have no knowledge about the senseless ego and its flawed process of reflection, then rationalization splits feelings from thoughts and undermines the powers of reason.

****

The ego's ability to control us comes from its cleverness to keep us in the dark and escape detection. Most of us have no awareness of its existence and have no realization of the many ways it is capable of manipulating us. We have no idea and no understanding of its ability to influence our thoughts and our actions, namely, what we feel, think, and do.

The ego's ability to possess and command our mind causes its beliefs and desires to be kept in the vanguard of our mind to influence every decision we make. We accept these decisions as hunches, premonitions, or a feeling in our bones.

These are gut feelings that come from the ego. And they are wrong because the ego is illogical and irrational. People mistakenly rely on gut feelings, because they do not understand the difference between gut instinct and intuition.

When you block the ego's thoughts, there is a second, little voice you can hear in your head called intuition. When the ego is barred from your mind, then you can utilize your intuition and make inquiries that will suddenly let you know a solution.

Intuition is also known as your Thought Adjustor, your Mysterious Monitor, your Holy Spirit, your Guardian Spirit, etcetera.[3] The description of the devil (your ego) on one shoulder and an angel (your intuition) on the other shoulder both whispering advice in your ears has some rationale to those who have grasped the importance of their intuition and allowed it to guide them. When you keep the ego's thoughts out of your mind with awareness, then intuition becomes a valuable asset, whereas gut feelings will lead you astray.

Within you resides; 1. You. 2. The ego. 3. The higher self. 4. The physical self. 5. The 'mind' or 'soul.' Now a sixth entity joins this group, which is your intuition. I believe your Intuition is an indwelling spirit that has a voice of its own. Your Intuition is not some vague, mysterious feeling, beyond comprehension; it is an actual spirit within you.

Intuition seems to be spiritual in nature, as some believe that their intuition is their Guardian Spirit. This seems to be a necessity to counterbalance the power and influence the ego has over us.

When you are aware you put up a firewall, that blocks the ego from entering, occupying, and controlling the mind, which then allowed you have access to both the rational half and the problem-solving halves of the neocortex. You now have, in addition, the right to make use of your intuition that the ego prevented you from doing because of its obsessive-compulsive desire to be thinking all the time.

The ego can put ideas into your mind that you would swear were coming from you and not the ego. The ego has the ability to sway your thinking with its own accounts or versions, which you will believe are your own and therefore are valid. None of the decisions made with the ego's influence will be correct, because they will guide you down a path of the ego's agendas, beliefs, and desires.

You will often make decisions that you will feel are right, but they feel right because the ego is so happy with your decisions. Therefore, you really need your intuition's guidance to countermand the influence of your ego.

Although we have willpower, the ego's powerful obsessive/compulsive, emotional drive gives the ego an exponentially unbalanced and unjust influence over us. So, Intuition can put us on a more equal footing with the ego to deal with all the hardships it creates in our life.

Intuition is here to help you deal with the problems and stresses of life. Since the ego is always in your head with thoughts you can't distinguish from your own, causing you to make selfish and unwise decisions for you, your intuition can retract and nullify those decisions and lead you on the proper and less foolish and stressful path.

Your intuition can only communicate with you when you are in control of your mind, in other words, when you're in the present. When the ego is in your head, thinking about the past or future, the ego puts up a firewall that effectively cuts off communications with your intuition. The ego does not like the entity I call, 'intuition,' and will try hard to inject its voice to override your intuition. When you are in the present, know that you are not alone, know that your intuition is always there as a guide to assist you with your decisions.

****

When we're aware, we're in the present. Our awareness and our attentiveness put up a firewall that blocks the ego's concerns about the past and the future. As soon as we try to observe the ego's thoughts, stop. The only way we know what the ego was thinking is by recalling its thoughts using memory. Just our awareness of the ego's thoughts will halt the ego from thinking to enable us to regain control of the mind.

Since we are unconscious when the ego is thinking, then the only way we know what the ego was thinking is by recalling the ego's thoughts using memory. Just our awareness of the ego's thoughts will halt the ego from thinking to enable us to regain control of the mind.

Pretend that you're a lion in the bushes awaiting prey (an ego's thought) to cross your path to pounce on it. When you try to observe the ego's thoughts, you have activated your power of awareness. This attentiveness makes you the leader because you have taken back your custody of the mind.

****

Awareness occurs when you have the intention to be aware. Awareness takes effort, mindfulness, will power, attentiveness, and self-discipline. Most of all, it's a skill you develop by practicing.

There are over three dozen behavioral tools that can keep the ego's thoughts out of your head, so you can maintain control of your mind. But all the behavioral instruments function primarily to enhance awareness.[1,2]

A sense of wonder and awe is a behavioral tool. If you look at the majesty of a mighty oak with a sense of wonder, you can experience a feeling of clarity, peace, or serenity, because the ego's thoughts have been blocked. The sensation of wonder puts up a barrier to the ego's ability to be in your mind, because it is a form of awareness.

Reading is one of the top major tools of awareness that you can use to secure the control of your mind. If you have trouble reading, then it's because the ego does not like you to read and will impede your ability to read by constantly injecting its thoughts while you read. You have to tell the ego that you're the boss and you will not put up with its interference any longer, and it will obey your order.

The ego's obsessive-compulsive motivational drive is exponentially stronger than your motivational drive or willpower. So, you are at a considerable disadvantage, if you try to compete and go head to head against the ego; it will win, and you will lose. But awareness swings the scales over to your side, allowing you to take command of your mind and control the ego.

Only the nuclei and neural pathways located in the limbic brain of the ego can create anger, hate, fear, and insecurity. The ego still needs access to your thoughts before these adverse stresses can affect you. Awareness blocks these negative feelings from having any impact. Awareness stops the ego's influence and control. However, once you give way and express the ego's drama, then the ego can easily and deftly manipulate you to suit its own needs and ends for its own benefit which then allows it to be in control of your mind. And this is when you are vulnerable to feelings of fear, anger, and insecurities.

When you've blocked the ego's thoughts and create a clear mind, this is not a passive state but is an active, energized state of being. When you can keep your mind clear of any thought by maintaining awareness, then you can gain command of both the neocortex of your brain's logical and rational abilities, and you gain access to the creative, problem-solving adeptness of the neocortical gray matter of the higher self in the brain's other hemisphere.

In other words, you have not only increased your intellectual capacity, but your judgment, reasoning, understanding, comprehension, and your wisdom. The ego will try to prevent that from happening and will try and prevent you from having a calm, peaceful mind that is free of worrisome thoughts.

For a thought to come from you requires effort, like when you are learning something, solving a problem, studying, planning, or creating something. Any of these efforts will block out the ego's efforts to be in your mind. When the easy and simple thoughts of the ego are in our head, we are not mindful of what's going on within us or around us. We should raise our level of consciousness by making an effort to become more aware.

We will never achieve genuine, emotional freedom until we are free of fear, we are free of anger, and we are free of insecurities. Those who are genuinely emotionally free will have no trouble establishing a stable, functioning, intimate relationship. The barrier to our freedom is the ego. Real emotional freedom will never happen until we acquire knowledge about the ego, understand the power of awareness, and realize that our rational, conscious self has the authority to tell the ego what it can do and what it cannot do! Who is going to control the mind! You or the ego. The one who occupies the mind is the one who will control the mind, and you control the mind with awareness.

Chapter 2

Three different nervous systems motor, sensory, or autonomic can influence the character and nature of the ego. The sensory nervous system handles incoming stimuli like sound, light, smells, touch, and taste that affect the senses. These stimuli travel from the external peripheral nervous system, bringing information into the central nervous system.

I'll refer to an ego with a dominant sensory nervous system, as the 'open' ego. The 'open' ego (sensory dominate) has a greater sensitivity that results in a person enjoying all the senses more than most.

The 'open' ego is like an antenna or sponge. The absorbent nature of the ego tends to make it more approachable and open-minded, relatively speaking.

Unfortunately, the 'open' ego can be quickly overwhelmed by excessive noise, light, sound, or hot spicy foods; and can have a low threshold for pain.

A person will often protect their 'open' ego by avoiding excessively stimulating situations and stressful people. It will avoid circumstances that it thinks are unnerving and steer clear of overstimulating conditions. To avoid tense and stressful situations, it has to be thinking ahead about what might happen.

****

Because the 'open' ego tends to worry about what might occur, anxiety and fear become its greatest problem. He or she may avoid people and seek refuge or escape from emotional distress and may search for solitude as a sanctuary.

When the 'open' ego is in charge of the mind, it will focus primarily on what could take place; specifically, it will be troubled with worry, anxiety, or fear. So, its mantra becomes 'What if?'

When you augment your anxiety, it takes the ego aback and stops it in its tracks. It startles the ego that you could take over its power to be afraid, and this reduces the fear and takes away the ego's ability to be in control while empowering you, which causes the ego to back off from creating fear and yield to your authority.

Anybody who allows the ego's thoughts to be obsessively concerned about the future is going to be easily frightened, and they will have to deal with this anxiety and fear created by the ego. Anybody who can stay in the present with awareness is not going to be afraid of anything that isn't life threatening, regardless of their nature or character.

The 'open' ego with a dominant sensory system has more mental energy compared to others. It can have more of a cerebral or intellectual edge over others, but only if you rule and can overcome the fears and stresses the ego creates. But when the 'open' ego is in control, then you will have the most difficult and most challenging ego of all to contain and keep under control, because the mother of all emotions is fear.

****

One of the behavioral tools that will alleviate the problems of living in the land of 'What if,' is just to stop breathing! Any time you suspend your breathing or hold your breath, you're in a hyper-vigilant or hyper-aware state. When you cease breathing, you will notice a sensation of serenity and peacefulness which envelopes you, because this action puts you in the 'present.' You're in the now moment, because awareness has stopped the ego's thoughts and it no longer controls your mind.

Holding your breath in abeyance is an important tool that you can use anytime and anywhere. Even at night when the ego's dreams stress you out. When you experience a terrible dream created by the ego, you can suspend your breathing to regain some rationality.

Negative stress, tension, or troubles that happened during the day can nag the ego, and it will review those situations in nighttime dreams. The ego believes these imagined dreams are real events, and even blame you for the tribulations and burdens that it experienced during a dream. You have to tell the ego that the dreams were not real. If you don't make this clear to the ego, it will believe the dreams were real events.

Dreams about bad past experiences or terrible future events are to stop! Your body is your temple in your kingdom, and you are the king! The ego needs to realize that you are the boss of the self, and the ego has to 'stop' dreaming on any subject you wish! Dreams that provide a solution to a problem you've been working on will come from the higher self.

Intimacy can be intimidating to the ego, as it wants to be independent, separate, and apart from others. When two people look into each other's eyes, the shyness of the ego will cause them to feel awkward or uncomfortable.

When you suspend your breath, the tension and nervousness created by the ego cease. When you discontinue breathing, you block the ego's thoughts, and a beautiful thing happens, as feelings of peace and calmness flow through you.

When you look into the eyes of someone and smile, you'll experience a feeling of confidence, as you allay the ego's nervousness with this behavior tool of delayed breathing.

When you just stop breathing, you enhance the possibility of establishing a relationship, simply because of the awareness that interrupting your breath created. By blocking the thoughts coming from the ego, this mindfulness alleviated the angst the ego felt about how threatening intimacy may become in the future. Denying the ego access to your mind, makes it extremely hard for the ego to be in charge.

****

The mouth, tongue, throat, and jaw are the ego's domain. When the 'open' ego is apprehensive, it can cause you to experience a hard swallow, a gulp, a dry mouth, jaw tension, clamped teeth, or choking.

When the ego experiences anxiety, fear, or anger, the tongue will tighten up and contract; this can cause you to feel tense or apprehensive. Many will chew gum to relax the ego and get some relief from this tension the ego creates around the mouth.

A behavioral skill to calm the ego is to expand the tongue, so it touches all the teeth and the roof of the mouth. Enlarging the tongue relaxes the tongue and throat area, which relaxes the ego. This expansion loosens the tongue and the throat area and calms the ego's apprehensive feelings to create a peaceful, 'alpha' brain wave pattern. Tranquility can come over you when the cells in the brain are firing together in unison and harmony in this 'alpha pattern' to put you in the 'zone,' in a state of 'Zen.'

****

Anger and fear come from the basolateral aspect of the ego's limbic brain.[1,2,3,4,5,6,7,8,9,10,11,12,13.] Your brain does not have the neural pathways or nuclear network to create fear, anger, or insecurity. When these occur, the ego is expressing its state of being. To arrive at this state, it needs access to your mind. If you block the ego's entry to your mind with awareness, you erode the

21

ego's influence, as it has lost most of its power to create these negative, stressful feelings.

****

The 'open' ego tends to project blame inward at you and be judgmental and critical of the things you do, say or think. When an 'open' ego's feelings are hurt, it will turn those feelings inward, blaming you and create feelings of regret, shame, guilt, despair, or depression to make you feel unworthy.

If you make a mistake, the ego will continually recall the memory of this blunder and harp back to it and magnify this slip of the tongue out of all proportions to undermine your confidence and weaken you. Casting aspersions at you usurps your authority and elevates the ego, so it is in control.

The 'open' ego will at times feel a rapport with someone else's troubles and absorb or feel the suffering they are experiencing and then blame you, making you feel guilty for these problems.

The 'open' ego tends to project blame inward towards you and be more judgmental and critical of the things you do, say, or think.

For those who feel isolated, this attitude by the ego if not corrected can lead to distress, sadness, depression, or suicide. So, do not let your ego get away with these put-downs of you, nor let it belittle you, nor make you feel guilty. The ego will put you down to let you know it is in charge and in control.

Do not let your ego get away with these put downs of you, nor let it belittle you, nor make you feel guilty. The ego will put you down to let you know it is in charge and in control.

You tell your ego silently, so no one can hear, "Stop it! You do not judge, evaluate, criticize, and punish the self! You accept us as is. You stop criticizing; you are not the captain, I am!" Demand that the ego follows your beliefs about life. You must put your foot down and steer the ego towards your views of life. Your goal is to insist the ego follow your lead by taking command of your authority.

****

The 'open' ego has a mentality that enjoys just being alone with a book. Reading can be stimulating and engrossing to the 'open' ego. Fresh information can combine with past experiences to generate new ideas. Creative thoughts and ideas will compulsively be repeated excitedly in your mind by the 'open' ego to cause it to disturb your ability to fall asleep and cause you to suffer the most with insomnia and become a night owl.

The ego has a tremendous amount of influence in your ability to fall asleep. The preoptic area of the ego's limbic brain is our sleep center[14,15,16.] How fast we fall asleep depends on the whims of the ego. You can suffer from insomnia if the ego has ideas and thoughts that it thinks are exciting and stimulating, by constantly putting these notions into your head. You do have the power to stop this and stops the ego from interfering with your sleep.

You are the commander-in-chief of the ego. You have the authority to order the ego to stop thinking when you're trying to fall asleep. If you're tired and sleepy, the ego will sabotage your sleep to engage in some exciting idea it wants to promote.

If the ego has thoughts to convey, the ego must restrict its notions to imagery. There will be no verbal thoughts! Verbal ideas in the form of words create high-frequency 'beta' brain wave patterns that are stimulating and interfere with sleep.

You get slower alpha wave activity with mental imagery that causes brainwave cells to fire in harmony as seen in the dreaming stage of sleep. Imagery induces an alpha brain wave pattern and a state of peace where you are more likely to fall asleep. These dreamlike visuals may involve people. With your insistence, the ego will start engaging in imagery and behaviors it can employ to help you fall asleep. Verbal thoughts create rapid, random, and stimulating thoughts of 'beta' brain wave activity.

****

Imagery is the ego's domain. You can only produce brief, fleeting images because the creation of imagery is not in your realm of abilities. A measure you can bring into play to aid sleep is to create a feeling of lassitude and inertia.

Sleep is not in the 'body's realm of abilities and will not be able to help you. You can tell or order the ego to engage in sleep, but if the sensory nervous system is robust in an 'open' ego, then this inherent quality can be difficult with the ego's capacity to assist you in falling asleep.

The heart chakra can offer some aid in sleeping. Creating a feeling of gratitude for the people you know and the things you have can bring the heart in to assist you and produce an inner harmony and a slower rhythm within the body.

****

A cat has a sensory nervous system that dominates the motor and autonomic nervous systems, and like a cat, the 'open' ego is going to be curious.

The 'open' ego's energy influences a person to become a professional student, librarian, intellectual, scholar, writer, researcher, scientist, or professor.

Chapter 3

The motor, sensory and autonomic nervous systems shape the ego's character or nature. This chapter deals with a motor, dominate nervous system, and its related ego type which I'll refer to as an 'adventurous' ego.

The 'adventurous' ego (motor dominate) enjoys outdoor activities, like exercising, camping, jogging, and hiking; it enjoys doing things by the 'sweat of the brow.'

The ego with a dominant motor nervous system projects out a responsive energy that travels from the central nervous system outward to the peripheral nervous system.

It projects blame to the outside world rather than take personal responsibility. The 'adventurous' ego blames the golf club or the gun, instead of itself.

The 'adventurous' ego is expressive and can be a charming actor. With abundant energy, it's the one most likely to keep its surroundings neat and tidy.

It is the motor neural pathways that pull information from storage in the central nervous system.[1,2,3.]

The 'adventurous' ego allows you to have a good memory, compared to others, because the 'adventurous' ego pulls data out from its memory bank located in the hippocampus.

Movement, exercising, or working out when you are trying to learn something amplifies the ability to memorize new information. You can create and maintain your memories better when you move around rather than remain sedentary. Students can perform better on academic tests if they move their bodies to solidify a retention loop of the information they have absorbed.

****

Awareness takes self-discipline and willpower. When we relax, lay back, and operate on automatic pilot, we hand over control of the mind to the ego. We have opened the mind and invited the ego to take over. When we lose awareness, then the 'adventurous' ego's thoughts will be about the past. It will recall past slights and retrieve memories of an emotional, hurtful nature.

The 'adventurous' ego tends to live in the land of 'if only.' 'If only' I had done this. 'If only' I had done that. You have to cope with feelings of regret about the past with the 'adventurous' ego. Guilt is a form of regret. Regret and guilt hold onto the past to ensure the ego's control. You are listening to the voice of the ego when you feel regret or guilt.

Once you assert your authority and achieve command of the mind, regret or guilt become superfluous, as you can be determined not to make that mistake again. Once you've resolved to avoid those problems, then there is no need to feel sorry, sad, lament, or other adverse stresses of regret and guilt created by the ego.

****

When the 'adventurous' ego recalls memories from former times, then it often creates feelings of grief, hurt, resentment, anger, or hate; also, you've allowed the ego to rule, because you've lost awareness. When the mind dwells in the past, then anger becomes a problem you need to handle.

The ego recalls a past slight, and it will make an assumption that it was personal and may even assume that it was an attack. Since the ego is not rational, it will believe that assumptions are facts. A suggestion can quickly become an assumption and then a fact by the ego. So, when you make an assumption, the ego will believe that it's a fact, and that is why you should avoid making assumptions.

When you allow the ego's thoughts to dwell in the past, you are going to have to deal with an angry ego. Awareness resolves this because it gets you out of the past and into the present. Previous hurtful remarks can get the ego upset and angry. These feelings can start to simmer, and with the ego's imagination, they can begin to boil.

Bad feelings stew, as the ego wants to resolve these past injustices. The ego will repeat some disturbing idea continuously until it wears you down and ruins your previous, comfortable attitude to create a very agitated, emotional state. The ego will replay these past events over and over again in your mind because the ego wants to realize some kind of retribution.

Not understanding that these negative emotions originate within the ego, many embrace them as a fundamental aspect of their inner self, that can lead to ideas of vengeance and getting even. A sense of rage in the ego can begin to take over. Unchecked anger coming from the ego can cause them to lose control. Loss of self-control combined with anger can lead to violence or even murder.

The ego's compulsive obsession for vengeance can overwhelm you and seem to be beyond your ability to contain them. Do not give up. This desire for revenge is a problem you have to handle. These feelings can be overwhelming and can cascade down out of control. So, learn the early warning signs coming from the ego so that you can interrupt the ego to take back control, and steer clear of trouble.

****

When you feel anger from the ego, you can count back by threes from three hundred. The effort to make this attempt can sidetrack the ego and allow you to take back control of the mind. Or you can just count to ten. This interruption of the ego's obsession provides time to calm your mind. When you count, you take possession of your mind, and this blocks the ego's thoughts to let you regain control of the mind.

The wrath of negative emotions is coming from the mindlessness of the ego. If you act on them, then you have relinquished your responsibilities as the one in charge of the self and have given over that job to the ego and let it be the boss so that it's in charge. You have handed over control and command of the self to an emotionally immature entity, your ego.

When you start to get hot under the collar, the ego is getting upset. Don't let it decide how you will conduct yourself. You want to be reacting appropriately and not let it rule and be your boss. Awareness of the ego's irritation makes you mindful of the ego's vexation and will allow you to avert or prevent an angry attack so that a calmer mind can prevail.

To the ego, resentment and anger are not feelings it enjoys but rather embraces. The ego thrives on drama; making a scene provides the ego easier access to your mind, and it covertly influences you to go along with its agenda.

****

When you just stop breathing, it makes you hyper-vigilant and is a behavioral skill that allows you to reclaim your mind. Another tool you can employ to deal with anger is to lighten your mood by not taking life so seriously. When you're serious in an emotional situation, you've allowed the ego to be in charge, so by 'letting go,' or when you 'lighten up' or 'accept life as it is,' you are asserting your authority.

The wish to control others is the main reason why anger emerges within a person. When you have a desire or an attitude to control another, that allows the ego to be your boss and causes you to become the ego's pawn. The desire to control others comes straight from the ego, and when the ego can persuade you to start controlling another, then anger coming from the ego can be easily aroused when they fail to do what you want, and you become the egos' puppet.

If you would rather not be an angry person, then you must put your foot down and state, "We do not impose or force our will on another to do our bidding. We do not dominate and force others to follow our beliefs and ideas." You have the power to change the ego, so it follows your attitude about life. The ego will go along with your views and establish you as the leader who's in control.

These behavioral skills can calm a situation down and allow you to approach the drama in a cool-headed way; these behavior skills put you in charge of the mind and lets you be the commander of the self.

****

To carry resentment or a desire for revenge is a bad belief system. The ego relishes and loves to replay a hateful situation, but it harms your psyche. You will pay a price when you relive situations involving harmful feelings. You start to live with bad feelings and emotional displeasure which influences you to become sarcastic in a mean-spirited way and cruel.

When you feel the ego's anger, and you act on it, you are displaying an emotional immaturity. You've become a tool of the ego. The more the ego's in charge, the more emotionally immature you will appear to others.

****

The best behavioral tool to control anger is forgiveness. The ego is incapable of forgiveness. So, you will never be able to forgive if the ego is in control. When you are in control, you can forgive. You are letting go of hurt when you learn to forgive. You are freeing yourself from the ego's emotional bondage and control over you.

Forgiveness does not change the past, but it changes the reality of the mind. When feeling vengeful, it's an opportunity to learn forgiveness and to let go of blame. Forgiveness has everything to do with you, and little to do with the offender and doesn't mean reconciliation. You forgive as a favor to yourself, not the offending party. You forgive to overcome one of the ploys or tricks the ego uses to control you.

Forgiveness is for your emotional and mental health. You will forgive to feel compassion for yourself. We were born with the ability to forgive. When you were a child, you could forgive right away. Two kids can be in a huge fight and a few minutes later, they are playing together again as if nothing has happened.

There is no other way to wipe out the pain of past emotional injuries created by the ego but forgiveness. You need to forgive those who have hurt you, even if it seems impossible to you. You forgive not because they deserve it, but because you don't want to suffer every time you remember what they did to you. You practice forgiveness until it becomes a habit.

****

The motor neural pathways suppress fear. The more the motor nervous system dominates, the more it inhibits fear in the brain.[4,5,6.] Some do not know what it is like to experience fear. So, the strong 'adventurous' ego type tends to be a risk taker, as it takes a little danger to excite it.

****

When the motor nervous system dominates in the ego, it can draw you into entrepreneurship, physical labor, sales, sports, public speaking, professional dancing, preaching, and acting.

Chapter 4

The motor and sensory nervous systems have been shown to have an impact on the ego's character. This section will describe the effect of the autonomic nervous system on the ego with its corresponding ego type described as the 'merging' ego.

The autonomic nervous system is what controls and regulates your internal organs or your viscera. When the autonomic nervous system is dominant in the ego, it provides an associative type of thinking pattern. Associative thinking is the mental process of 'relationship thinking' and learning by making associations between a subject and present circumstances.

The 'merging' ego tends to be socially active and would rather be with people than be alone. So, the 'merging' ego tends to merge, mingle, and blend with others. The 'merging' ego has a gut reaction to life. Its associative thinking pattern is mainly concerned with ordinary, everyday, practical matters. It tends to strip away vague abstractions. This ego type goes right to the heart of a matter and knows what it wants to do. The 'merging' ego wants you to rely on its own perceptions, rather than take advice from others.

The 'merging' ego is not bothered much by anger or fear but is troubled with feelings of insecurity. Uncertainties created by the ego about its status or standing of acceptance in relation to others in a vertical social position produces feelings of self-doubt, uneasiness, and tension. Insecurity and a lack of confidence is something you want to put an end to and eliminate.

The 'merging' ego will judge and criticize others and you. It will rank people and you along a vertical social status hierarchy as being above or below the self, but rarely on the same level. The 'merging' ego will rate others and you as acceptable, or unacceptable, worthy, or unworthy, etc.

When you hear a judgment of disapproval in your head, it originates from the ego. When this criticism goes unchecked, it will come back to haunt you. You begin to question your worthiness and just how acceptable you are. This criticism or censure creates an alienated environment internally and externally, rather than a supportive environment or milieu.

The 'merging' ego will always include you in its ranking system. Its incriminations can undermine your confidence. The 'merging' ego is on guard to maintain and not lose social rank and self-esteem in the eyes of others and thus it will blame you when it feels this has occurred. Thus, the 'merging' ego can be in your head making you feel vulnerable, inhibited, and insecure.

****

These critical assessments by the 'merging' ego are what sabotages relationships. When a person experiences a failure in a relationship or a failure in marriage, then free rein has been given to the 'merging' ego to evaluate, classify, judge, and criticize one's significant other. Be aware that when you allow your ego to think in this critical manner without correction, you have given away your authority and permitted the ego to rule you and influence how you think.

When the ego starts criticizing others by thinking they are dumb, fat, crude, etcetera, it is sabotaging personal relationships and it has to stop. This judgmental attitude is how the ego insidiously brings about a steady decline in a relationship. This surreptitious undermining of a consort empowers the ego, but it will unwittingly create a dysfunctional partnership. The ego's propensity to find fault can be seen within members of a family to produce the same controlling, critically judgmental conditions that are the malignant roots of a dysfunctional family.

To counter this, you have to step up and say silently, "Hey! We don't judge and criticize anyone! This person has attributes that are praise-worthy and should be admired. Each person deals with life's journey in their way, in their own time. Each person learns by making their mistakes and needs to work out their challenges in life."

Alternatively, you can project love or gratitude towards this person. A feeling of thankfulness towards this person will countermand the ego's critical, single-minded belief system of critiquing and criticizing another to feel superior.

You should not tolerate the ego's judgmental and critical behavior for one second. The more you allow the ego to criticize others, the more you will suffer from feelings of insecurity. The 'merging' ego needs to change its way of thinking to be tolerant and accepting of other people and their personal view of life. You, as the director, can demand that the ego obeys you. You direct the 'merging' ego to start embracing life as it is, to start accepting people as they are! When you allow the ego to criticize another, it's going to come back and make you feel insecure.

The 'merging' ego has a lot of inertia that you have to manage. When you allow the ego to rule, this inertness will cause you to be resistant to change and this can generate a tendency for you to be stubborn. This inertia will also cause you to procrastinate and put things off and be the reason you arrive late to meetings or to appointments. As much as you love to party, you may be the last to arrive at a social gathering.

This inertia can impede learning and growing, and can easily get you stuck in a rut. Since the 'merging' ego thinks life is just fine, it's unlikely to examine or explore new, exciting, and beneficial areas of life. It is often difficult to get the 'merging' ego excited or motivated to do anything, and it may cause you to lounge about and become a 'couch potato.'

If you, the rational self, do not take control and reject the 'merging' ego's slovenly outlook on life, then it may eventually lead to emotional, physical, or financial poverty.

The 'merging' ego, your engine of energy, requires you to make an effort to overturn the ego's lethargy. You must tell the 'merging' ego to improve the self, to develop, to learn, to expand, etcetera. You are the parent who needs to tell the ego, what it needs to do, and how it needs to be. The 'merging' ego is required to follow your demands and instructions. Remember that you are the director who controls the ego. You are the commander-in-chief, so what you tell the ego to do, it must obey. You inform the ego in no uncertain terms what you want it to do, and this will help you achieve your intentions and goals.

The 'merging' ego's inertia causes one to be socially nonchalant. It prefers to be socially involved with others, and its inertia conserves emotional energy, so, one can party all night long compared to the 'open' sensory ego who may be exhausted within an hour. The 'merging' ego wants, more than any other type, to settle down and cultivate family ties and establish roots in a family.

Herding animals like cows, pigs, sheep, and elephants have a dominant autonomic nervous system. Herding animals have a lot of bickering and infighting which creates a vertical, social hierarchy that establishes each member's rank in the group.

Because the 'merging' ego is social and good with people and wants the power to influence and control others, it influences a person to become a salesman, a manager, or a CEO. The 'merging' ego also craves the admiration of others, which allows them to increase their status rank of acceptance. This desire for status and position will draw them into the field of local and national politics and acting.

****

The 'merging' ego's judgments and criticisms of others also causes the ego to reevaluate and make assumptions and imaginings about your social position of respect in the eyes of others. The 'merging' ego makes speculations about its position and believes you are the reason for a rise or fall in its rank. This persistent evaluation and judgment of the self creates an emotional roller-coaster ride of ups and downs in your life. On the ride down, the 'merging' ego' can create a state of apathy, helplessness, or depression. The 'merging' ego's inertia can lock you into a state of melancholy. This quagmire is a situation that you need to recognize and correct.

The 'merging' ego's pathological problems will be emotional, namely of a manic/depressive, bipolar nature. Taken to the extremes, when you have allowed the 'merging' ego to have an extreme amount of control of your mind, it can go from the grandiosity of egomania to the misery and despair of a deep, dark depression. During the high side, the 'merging' ego displays a superior, domineering, snobbish, or conceited attitude, 'I'm better than you.'

Throughout this hot-blooded, manic phase, the 'merging' ego is in almost total control of the thoughts coming into the head. The ego will make foolish decisions for immediate gratification without regard for the consequences.

The seductive, euphoric, superior feelings of this high are so enticing, that without understanding what is happening, one can surrender to this 'high' or these feelings of elation and willingly go along with the thoughts coming from the ego.

Be aware of the consequences of these momentary, pleasurable highs, as it eventually leads to self-destructive behavior. During these happy times, the ego is illogical and irrational and wants only to satisfy its desires immediately, which creates a lot of harm to the family, friendships and loved ones.

To pull out of this notice at the beginning of these manic feelings, you may recognize a nervous ache, a flutter of nervousness, agitation, trembling, quivering, or butterflies in the pit of your stomach. Even though it's early on, these feelings can still be overwhelming and hard to control.

The behavioral tools that will allow you to regain control are to take a deep breath, then hold it. Tighten the belly by pushing downward, referred to as 'bearing down.' You can maintain this behavior by shallow breathing where you expand the chest and raise the shoulders when taking a breath.

Breathing in the upper chambers of the lungs will permit you to maintain downward pressure on the lower parts of the lungs. These behaviors produce tension. To relax, expand the tongue, so it touches the roof of the mouth. Relax the higher self by staring with awareness while you hold your breath and 'bear' down. These behavioral tools allow you to regain control of your thoughts so that you can get back to a state of normalcy.

****

This set of behavioral tools can also be applied to another problem that's experienced as an impotent, empty, washed out sense in the pit of the stomach. The 'merging' ego's attitude and belief in a hierarchy of acceptance creates feelings of inadequacy. The sensation of personal and emotional deficiency generates a drained feeling. You can triumph over the ego's sense of inferiority and revitalize your spirit by using the same techniques just explained that curtailed the ego's sense of superiority.

****

Some egos may be influenced by two nervous systems equally, while some may have a balance between all three nervous systems. The 'body' is an independent entity with its own belief systems but operates at the unconscious level. The body, the higher self, the ego, and you are each influenced by the motor, sensory, and autonomic nervous systems in independent ways. The interactions of these four entities, each controlled by separate nervous systems within you, can have many different and distinct emotional, personality, and character effects.

We are very complicated. Self-realization can cause some of us to have a hard time getting to know ourselves and getting along with ourselves. It is not easy to achieve self-realization. The complexities involved in understanding and dealing with our inner being can be troubling. It is difficult but ultimately important that we try and figure out, who we are and what we should do in life.

A relationship can magnify these problems. A relationship is going to be an interaction of eight different entities (four from each individual) that will need to get along with each other.

Each person in a relationship first has to understand their own complex nature. Getting to know yourself and how you function best will help give you the insight into how another may live out their own purpose in life.

An intimate relationship between two people with their many selves can be daunting, so knowledge about who you are, and what you want to do in life

34

helps in creating a stable relationship. This rationality holds true for friends and family as well. Knowing yourself and how you function is an important aspect to achieve lasting friendships and relationships.

Chapter 5

A culture will always create two social systems that conflict with each other. I'll refer to these two social networks as Status and Synergy. Each lies at the opposite end of a continuum or line, so one system operates at the expense of the other.

The Status social system emerges and evolves to satisfy personal desires. Their efforts are directed toward service to the self, or to those who want society to benefit the self. The Status structure is preferred by people who want to improve, evolve, and perfect the self. Improving the self is the primary desire of the ego. So, Status is an ego-driven culture.

At the opposite end of this span is the Synergy social system. Synergy is structured around people who want to serve others, namely those who want to care, aid, comfort, and help others. Synergy requires a rational, creative mindset that looks beyond the self to connect with others, nature, and the world which is beyond the boundaries of what the ego is interested in doing or achieving.

Nature is drawn to a 50/50 state of equilibrium or balance. However, a sixty percent state of service to others and a forty percent state of service to the self seems to be an ideal state for many. But the proportionality does not matter as much as the quality; so, that service to the self should encompass more knowledge and wisdom while service to others should embrace more tolerance, respect, and acceptance of others.

A Status system creates a social hierarchy of acceptance, referred to as a pecking order. A Status culture judges and classifies us by insinuation, innuendo, and gossip to determine how worthy and how acceptable we are.

Competition within a vertical ranking for a social position of respect and importance ensues, so one advances at the expense of another to decide just how suitable we are to be a part of a group, or whether we qualify to be a part of a particular class of people. The slings and arrows of a Status culture tends to undermine each other rather than support each other.

****

Ruth Benedict discovered a common characteristic or quality she referred to as 'Synergy,' that ran throughout the different primitive cultures she studied.[1]

'In societies with low Synergy (high Status), every act that was to the advantage of the individual was a victory over another. There were strong beliefs in the ability of power to defeat and humiliate others.

In these very competitive societies, each would take what he could get. This rivalry often took the form of heaping up goods in competition, and sometimes even letting them rot, rather than share them with others.

The people in these competitive Darwinian societies were revengeful, acquisitive, jealous, and anxiety ran throughout their community.

Real power was believed to reside in those who could inflict the most harm; while those who did the right thing by helping others had no power at all.

They developed powerful gods whom they feared. They trembled in the presence of these gods, who used punishment and vengeance.

Members of tribes with high Synergy greatly prized their personal skills, because any ability that was for the good of the individual was at the same time good for the group, where members supported each other in a kind of social solidarity.

Private possessions were treasured because they could be shared with others. Since everyone was provided for, there was no fear of poverty.

Anxiety was missing to the degree that seemed incredible to Benedict and her colleagues. These were societies of good will, where murder and suicide were virtually unknown.

They had kind gods with benign spirits whom they had no fear of and brought benefits and protected them.[1,]'

Status compels us to compete for acceptance, to avoid rejection and to avoid appearing unworthy in the eyes of others. We can gain approval and acceptance by improving ourselves. We raise our rank or position by showing or proving how much better we are than others.

The ego's nature is to judge and criticize the endless minute differences in people. This discrimination tends to create divisions within groups of individuals, instead of unity. It generates a vertical stratum that achieves the kind of Status environment where the ego can thrive, as it wants to be independent, separate, and apart from others.

In a social status culture, much effort and energy are spent trying to best others, to gain acceptance, and to move up the Status ladder. Status competitiveness for acceptance will keep us armed, guarded, and stressed.

Those in authority use rules, customs, traditions, and conventions as a method to control others and further their agenda and status. Status needs conformity to maintain a limitation on the aggression it creates. Obedience and compliance within a Status community pave the way for those in power to accomplish the outcomes they desire.

Status cultures create greedy people. Social rank is determined by the quality and quantity of goods people own. Individual possessions and wealth not only achieve the acceptance they need, but it's also a measuring stick of their worth and rank.

The stress created by a Status culture produces confusion about what is essential in life. Many believe fame can achieve the acceptance they so strongly desire. Others spend their time on social media to accumulate 'likes' and 'friends' to prove to themselves and others that they are worthy. Putting their worthiness in the hands of the many egos they are surrounded by every day, allows the ego to gain access to their minds. This confusion about their worth allows the ego to control them.

Social Status relies on discrimination by the ego to produce a ranking to divide people. It makes them vulnerable, insecure and pressures them to play by the rules and conform. A vertical, social, Status hierarchy results in an ego-dominated culture that is socially flawed and emotionally immature.

A person with beliefs in the authority of the Status system wants to influence, dominate, and control others. Status culture uses force and constraint rather than collaboration and communication to achieve its goals, as cooperation is not worth the effort nor necessary. This form of governance reveals another major flaw in a Status culture, and allows a marriage between corporations and government, which is one definition of Fascism.

****

Synergy's social culture creates a tolerant, flat structure, where everyone is deemed to have value and worth. All individuals and their behaviors are accepted. Synergy provides us with a secure, supportive environment so that we are free to achieve our intentions and goals, free to be creative, innovative, and productive. In a Synergistic society, there is less need for control and force, as life is acknowledged as it is, and people are accepted as they are.

****

A Status way of life discourages us from using our mental abilities. A mindless conformity is encouraged that makes us dependent on experts, government, corporations, marketing ads, and all the different forms of media, to tell us what to do, think, and feel. Those in control loathe public education but do encourage private or charter schools to advance the governing class.

A Status environment uses warnings, threats, and force to get people to work together. They need a humble, obedient, compliant and dependent population. They need followers. Confident, self-sufficient people with personal power produce conflicts and power struggles that challenge those in charge with alternative ideas and options.

As Status becomes more deeply entrenched, the need for threats and force becomes increasingly more and more blatant than the use of reason. The German Nazi regime and orthodox religious sects like the Sharia Law aspect of Islam, and the Ultra-Orthodox Judaism communities all require an extreme, vertical, discriminating, ranking system to enforce their control and authority.

The more extremely Status is established and ensconced in a culture, the more dominant the ego will be with its control of people's minds and thoughts. And the more the people will be plagued with a loss of personal freedom because they will be afflicted with the ego's nature of creating feelings of fear, anger, and insecurity. So, although these cultures may advance intellectually, productively, and technologically, their social development, which can make these advancements secure and robust, will be operating at a low or base level of development.

The ego wants to be independent and separate from others. Status achieves this for the ego by creating a state of rank, inequality, and separation among people. A pyramid of acceptance divides people and ranks them, so they are unequal and separate. Those at the top are entitled to acceptance from all those below. Those at the bottom of this social pyramid do not have the right to any approval from those above.

Just as there is a feeling of alienation for those near the bottom of this acceptance pyramid, there is a sense of insecurity for those at the top, because they have to be on guard to protect their position of rank and esteem in the eyes of others. The captain of the high school football team and the head cheerleader could feel their status was threatened if they were seen hanging with those at the lower levels.

Those at the bottom of this acceptance pyramid fester with the unjustness, intolerance, and hatred to create a contempt for society. The unfairness of life, created by this mean-spirited Status system, corrupts the innocence, integrity, morality, decency of our youth. Status can change the meaning of their life into one of hopelessness so that their only expectation for survival has to rely on their ability to take advantage of others, by grifting, stealing, deceiving, and bilking others.

This virulent Status social system can even influence actions of violence towards others. When we accept and live by an emotionally flawed Status system, everything that happens to us is a result of our efforts and beliefs, such as materialism, covetousness, acquisitiveness, avarice, and greed. We reap what we sow.

Status people celebrate the unfairness of life, and they thrive when it has an enemy it can hate. Only under Status will we find the subculture of homelessness. Many of the Status leaders are unjust, unkind and unfeeling to the poor and the unfortunate people while they become more materialistic, covetous, acquisitive, power hungry, and greedy. They remain in power, because they appeal to the envious egos of those who voted for them. When we accept and live by an emotionally flawed Status social system, everything that happens to us is a result of our own efforts and beliefs.

****

A vertical Status society allows the ego to thrive and be in control. The ego rules when you are stressed out with negative emotions, like anger, fear, and insecurities. When the ego occupies the mind most of the time, it creates problems at all relationship levels, whether within an individual, a couple, a group, community, a state, or a nation. A Status environment will be at the bottom rung of social development, because of the significant influence of the ego, even though these cultures may be advanced intellectually or technologically.

****

This Status system also holds true for American corporations with their top-down management style that produced unhappy workers. Employees of the Japanese automobile industries were encouraged to develop Synergetic relationships with their leaders. Their employees felt their co-workers were like family and would often forego vacations, as they loved working at their job.

Evolution favors the cooperative system of support that Synergy creates. Cooperation requires some give and take. It concedes a point or a position to compromise and come to some agreement. When we see a group of people come together, and use their problem-solving abilities, logic, rationality, and creativity and reach an agreement, it can result in a successful endeavor.

Quantum physics shows that the mental energy from our intentions can generate an invisible force that is capable of shaping matter. A group of people with similar intentions can combine forces to maximize results that are suitable for any group of individuals.

Status utilizes control and force rather than persuasion and cooperation. So, working together with others to bring about collaboration is a waste of time to them. To control others, they have to resort to intimidation and force. When ordinary, everyday folks defy the command of those in charge, it evokes anger. The authority figure naturally will react in an emotionally immature way, because of the ego's compulsive energy drive to control and retaliate on those who don't comply.

So, the culture of Status creates an emotionally immature reaction which leads to other emotionally immature behaviors. A Status structure is a macho system that produces low quality thinking that becomes a contagion that makes intimidation easier than reason, which can then regress to a lower level so that force is more convenient than cooperation.

Those with a desire to control others have become a puppet of the ego. The ego has a passion and a drive to control others. If they accede to the will of their ego and try to control others, they've become a tool of the ego, and they're ensconced in the Status social system. You have no rational need to control others. The desire to control others is a yearning of the ego because of its feelings of deficiency and incompetence and to compensate for its inability to rule the self. The more the ego is in control, the more the ego will influence him or her to act in an emotionally immature manner. So, when others don't accede to their desire, then the childish reaction of anger is the result.

****

There is an attitude of 'certainty' that shuts out other possibilities, such as cooperation and collaboration. 'Certainty' is a threat to creative thinking. An orientation towards 'certainty' is a need of the ego because it believes all assumptions are facts, and it wants its beliefs to be accepted.

A viewpoint of 'certainty' needs a scapegoat to protect its position or opinion and will focus feelings of aggression or hostility on this scapegoat. Scapegoating may be applied to genders, religions, people of different races, nations, sexual orientations, people with different political beliefs, or people differing in behavior from the majority.

The need to be 'right' is the result of the ego trying to protect the image it wants to project to the outside world. The ego has to impose its way of thinking, not just onto others, but also upon ourselves. An attitude of 'certainty' closes our mind to make us biased, intolerant and controlling. The belief systems of those who think they are always right, lose flexibility like all authoritarian type dogma. 'Certainty' by those in power can lead to war.

We should keep an attitude of doubt about our lives and our beliefs. We should be flexible about our beliefs and about what works in our lives. Many believe that scientific studies, often paid for and published by corporations to achieve an advantageous, beneficial, or profitable result is corrupted, and is often accepted as an absolute truth, like a religious belief, and take priority over rational and logical thinking. But logical, rational arguments should have an influence or an effect on our belief systems. To close our minds to sound judgments that employ reason, rationality, creativity, and common sense indicate the weakness 'certainty' creates.

****

It's alright to be 'serious' when you're alone and want to develop some technical expertise. The ego, your engine of energy, provides the vitality you need when you want to master some talent, ability, skill, or execute some technique free of faults. But if you're 'serious' when interacting socially with others, then you've invited the ego into an area where it lacks the social skills to be in charge. Seriousness engenders inappropriate emotions and critical judgments that create awkwardness. That's why Synergy operates with beliefs that say '*Che Sera Sera*,' or 'what will be, will be.' 'Accept things as they are.' 'Let go,' 'lighten up,' 'accept life as it is,' 'let it be,' or 'it is what it is.' This lighter attitude about life is an important behavioral tool when interacting socially. Recent research has provided evidence that mood can spread from person to person via a process known as social contagion.[2] So, when you're around people who are happy, you will tend to be happy.

Being grim and dour when dealing with others brings forth the ego's desire for control into play. Being serious can devolve into petty, immature feelings toward others when they don't accede to the rules the ego believes are important.

People in lower income bracket can be just as happy as those in a higher income group. The most important external factor is not a difference in income, but in our relationships. There are relationships at work, in our communities with neighbors, in our errands when we shop. But relationships suffer when we no longer trust the people we come in contact with on a daily basis.

Status influence among people has created a lack of trust in other people. There has been a profound cultural change caused by Status individualistic culture that created more stress and competition relative to the cooperation that is seen in Synergy. So, Status makes other people more of a threat to us and causes a lack of trust between people that has doubled in today's culture.

Synergy provides mutual support and acceptance among those in a synergetic group. Mutual acceptance creates a sense of belonging to the individuals, friends, families, and communities involved with Synergy, in contrast to the prejudice and inequality found in the vertical ranking of a Status group of people. Synergy creates a feeling of family and belonging and helps curtail aggression. This allows the more stimulating and creative environment of multiformity where eccentric, harmless behaviors are acceptable.

****

'The Nordic Theory of Everything: In Search of a Better Life' by Anu Partanen, shows how the Scandinavian governments form partnerships with citizens, business, and the public to work together. Her book demonstrates how this kind of cooperation can create a 'smart' government that creates a fair society that leaves it citizens free to lead innovative, happy, and productive lives.

She illustrates how the Scandinavian countries are the ones who have a government of the people, by the people, and for the people. America, by contrast with its revolving doors between government and corporations that operate for motives that do not benefit the public, but gives significant preference to businesses, corporations, and conglomerates. When companies become more important than people, it creates a big, world-wieldy government of the corporations, by the corporations, and for the corporations, where the middle class is affected by widening income disparity.

Our government's lack of collaboration with the people has created a toxic, greedy, partisan political climate that sabotages our growth with stubborn obstructions, public shutdowns, and harms our overall well-being as a nation. The foundation of those in power to rule is based on living a lie and then convincing others that that lie is the truth. The real threat to their power is truth. They rage against the Scandinavian forms of government because they wish to perpetuate their vertical status and rank to keep people down and under control.

She debunks criticism that Nordic countries are socialistic 'nanny states.' She shows that it is we Americans, with our ego-driven legislature, who are far more enmeshed in unhealthy dependencies.

The governments of the Nordic countries collaborate with their citizens to provide an open and transparent society. They have created and enjoy an environment that blesses their citizens with much more individual freedom, justice, and equality. The five Nordic countries are consistently shown to be the happiest with their lives when compared to other nations, and their education system consistently ranks in the top ten in math, language, and science.

In the Scandinavian countries, you have a trust level that is double what is found in other countries because they put more emphasis on cooperation and mutual respect. They have gravitated toward a more synergistic society with higher levels of trust. And this is why they feel happier than other nations.

A Synergetic society produces tolerance, acceptance, and therefore trust of their fellowman and overcomes the influence of the ego. The result is that Synergy yields a more socially mature, functional, and secure culture. Synergy opens up the higher mental functions of logic, rationality, and creativity within cultures, families, relationships, and within the self.

****

If Synergy could be encouraged and developed in our school systems, it would help eliminate the bullying problem. It would encourage students to help each other out because students helping other students is an excellent teaching device. It would create an environment where kids could look forward to going to school. It would allow the teacher to concentrate and help the needier student who is having a hard time. An environment of acceptance and unity that Synergy creates would eliminate most discipline problems.

****

Synergy can operate in tandem with hierarchies in the medical, economic, education, and entertainment realms. Technology and intellectual hierarchies can work alongside Synergy to allow them to thrive best in an environment of social support and acceptance, as can be seen operating in the Japanese automakers.

When Status hierarchies operate without gratitude, tolerance, and acceptance of the people involved in an organization, then you influence a mean-spirited, subversive, or obstructive type of environment, where people take advantage of others, instead of working together.

****

When you achieve excellence in a certain field by developing 'service to the self' while at the same time engaging in the acceptance and tolerance of other people, characteristic of 'service to others,' then this orientation that unites these two disparate services, removes the conflicts and lessens the differences between people. This breaks down the barriers between people by joining others together to create an atmosphere of bipartisanship and collaboration. The success of a relationships depends on whether people are oriented toward cooperation or control, aligned with Synergy or with Status. Those who want control, use relationships as a steppingstone for advancement. Synergy creates an emotional connection with others to give life more meaning, as mutual support and acceptance create a happy and productive life.

As long as the ignorance about the ego continues within a culture, the dysfunctional Status social system will prevail. When there is no knowledge about the ego, then the stress-producing behaviors of Status will triumph over the moral codes of Synergy.

The reason for this is that the ego is more vigilant than you are because it is entirely sure of its purpose. The ego knows what it wants, and will go after it with its obsessive-compulsive drive. Without knowledge about the ego, with its drive to control, with its drama for critical divisiveness, and with its desire to be independent and separate, the ego will win with its competitive arguments for Status. And Status will rule because of the ego's obsessive-compulsive drive, the length of time it possesses the mind, and the lack of awareness of how much this immature entity controls us.

The only times Synergy can be seen operating among people in our culture are the few weeks before Christmas, as acceptance and trust become rampant. The question is, which world do you want to live in? Under Status where the ego's desire for separation, stress, and strife can prevail, or the state of Synergy where knowledge about the ego can create a friendlier state that encourages a sense of connection, acceptance, and belonging to become the norm?

Chapter 6

Love is a relaxing stimulate. It is the most powerful behavioral tool in our arsenal. Love can keep the ego out of our heads. Love is so powerful that it's the one behavioral tool that can hold a couple together and create a functional and stable family. Those who have pondered life's meaning know that we do not live only for ourselves but live for others and all life. We should be inspired to live a moral and virtuous life for others and set an example for others to follow.

Love should be unconditional. Conditional love brings the ego into the mix. Emotional insecurity places conditions on love. Unconditional love doesn't mean you've become enslaved. When someone no longer meets your needs, you can leave in love instead of leaving in anger and hate.

****

Infatuation is a romantic attraction, indulged and driven by the ego. Many egos are captivated by a beautiful face or body, the sensual pleasures of sex, celebrity, or fame, or by those who create exceptional music or food. Infatuation can be mistaken for 'love' and can make 'love' seem fickle or fleeting.

The limitations of infatuation are that beauty fades and senses become sated. After familiarity sets in, various problems are discovered with habits and compatibly. Once difficulties appear, then the ego's desire to be separate begins to prevail. Without knowledge about the ego's desire for control, the ego starts to judge and criticize variant behaviors in another. Overcoming these judgments by the ego can take a major amount of effort and energy.

The love between two people curbs the ego's judgmental and critical nature. However, once their love starts to wane, the barrier that kept the ego's thoughts at bay, now weakens and allows the ego's troublesome, divisive ideas to be brought into the union.

As the ego begins to judge and critically pick apart the significant other's imperfections, differences, and disparate behaviors, it starts a downward spiral of judgments and criticisms, creating frictions that can cause even soulmates to break up.

Personal demons, also known as emotional immaturities, create problems as the ego's opinions, thoughts, and criticisms, give us doubts and second thoughts about our mate.

Breakups result primarily from a lack of awareness that the ego exists as a separate, independent entity and a dearth of understanding of its abilities and beliefs. This lack of knowledge of the ego allows its attitudes to suppress our ideas and convictions. We need to recognize what the ego is doing and reclaim our real values, rather than allow the ego's petty nature to undermine our relationships with its values.

We are conscious of the ego's criticisms, but think that it's a part of our inherent, true nature. When you let the ego's criticisms slip by critically unnoticed or unchecked without any rational thought, then by neglect, you've sanctioned the ego's beliefs with a disregard for the value of your judgment. This false reality resides in those with no knowledge of the ego. Rejection of these erroneous beliefs would be automatic from those who have knowledge and understanding about the ego.

When the ego is in your mind, it will rule with its low quality, irrational thoughts, and cause you to believe these are a valid assessment of your feelings about a relationship. It is important to understand that these feelings are not coming from you, they are coming from the immaturities of an ego who desires to be independent, separate, and apart.

****

You are made up of different entitles, each with its own particular vibrational frequency. These individual, distinct beings can be referred to as you, the higher self, the soul, the ego, and the body. The vibrational frequency of each of these selves can combine to make up the overall harmonic, vibrational frequency of a person.

When another person vibrates with a harmonic overtone in sync with your overall frequency, you will experience a comfortable rapport with that person. The closer the vibrational match, the more it will create seamless conversations, and easy laughter. There can be a mutual sense of purpose, a feeling of emotional security, and a lack of self-consciousness. When two individuals are 'in tune,' then the relationship is in harmony, and actions and nuances seem to need no explanation. This harmonic connection makes everything easy and can create an enduring love, which goes beyond the limitations of infatuation.

47

****

Love arises from our spiritual nature. Love is an innate connection felt with another or others. Love springs forth from an understanding that all things have a spiritual aspect, so everything has a connection. All is one.[1]

All objects are made up of energy in the form of atoms. A table is an inanimate object and is inorganic, but in a spiritual sense, it is alive! The table is made up of atoms with electrons spinning around the nucleus to create an electromagnetic field that surrounds it. People are also made up of atoms and have an electromagnetic field that surrounds them. Collectively, all these atoms and energy fields create an aura with its unique frequency. Once you realize there is spiritual connection with all life, you create a relationship with life. You increase the possibility that love can become a part of all living things.

A plant was attached to a lie detector with a paper printout that recorded its responses. A leaf was hooked up to the machine, and when it was about to be cut with some scissors, the needle moved up and down wildly just before it was to be cut with scissors; indicating the plant had extrasensory perception because it was conscious of this person's intentions.

A person came into a room with two plants. This person then destroyed one of the plants. The next time this same individual entered the room, the needle on the graph went up and down like crazy, showing the spirit of that plant had an awareness of who this terrible and dangerous person was! ('The Secret Life of Plants,' by Tompkins and Bird)

If you tell a plant every day, "I love you," that plant will flourish and thrive. If you tell a plant daily, "I hate you," that plant will do poorly and whither.[2,3]

A tree, a flower, or a plant has a consciousness that is aware of any love you project toward it. You create love when you feel a spiritual link with another person or nature. This ethereal attachment is the foundation on which love can grow. When you feel this spiritual connection, and provide comfort to another or nature, this is to your spiritual self as physical exercise is to your body.

****

Love is the domain of the higher self. Love emanates from the higher self. But your ability to love depends on you! If you wait for the higher self to create a loving feeling, it's not likely to happen. How loving a person you are, is dependent on you, the logical, rational self. Your intention to be loving as the director of the self helps determine whether love will be expressed or not by the higher self.

You elicit loving feelings from the higher self by connecting with other energy forms or spirits. When you feel you're one with a plant, an animal or a human, this connection will cultivate feelings of love, which is the foundation for a relationship. This spiritual union or sense of oneness is the basis on which you can experience love.

Love is not a notion; it results from a deliberate effort. To be happy, you have to love, you have to experience love. But if you don't love yourself, you cannot be happy, and that self-love has to be unconditional. If you don't love yourself, you won't be able to love others. You have the authority to command the higher self to follow your intentions. Love is manifested within the high self. Since the eyes are the domain of the high self, then if you desire to feel loving, you need to soften and relax the eyes to encourage the higher self to be loving, along with a slight smile with the cheeks. Your directive to be more loving is an exercise to strengthen your ability to love. To be a master of love, you have to practice being loving.

Self-love occurs when you love the higher self, the 'body,' and the ego. This self-love has to be unconditional. If you don't love yourself, you won't be able to love others. To love yourself and others, you have to practice, practice, practice!

****

As your skills of awareness grow, you may experience loving feelings welling up from within for no reason. There is a reason, your efforts to reduce the ego's drama and stress has allowed the higher self to enjoy a peaceful tranquility. The higher self feels more protected and more enthused about life and is pleased with your efforts.

Like the words of a song say, 'Put a little love in your heart, and the world will be a better place.' Bringing your intention to be loving to the forefront of your thinking is like a command to the higher self to be more loving. The song, 'Making love out of nothing at all' by Air Supply, is a feeling you can generate within yourself if you can feel the spiritual connection with nature, others, and the world around you. And Jesus said in the book 'A Course in Miracles,' "When you make an error or a mistake, it is because of a lack of love in your thinking."

****

I believe spirits will strive to grow. When a person incarnates into a physical form, his rate of growth can increase exponentially, because of all the challenges and the catalysts that the ego and the physical world presents. The ego does not exist in the spirit world. When you physically incarnate, you have to learn how to overcome the stress, anger, fear, insecurity, physical pain, etcetera, that the ego generates. To learn how to overcome and vanquish the emotional, mental, physical, and spiritual pain created by the ego is the main reason a person makes the transformation from the spiritual world and materialize in a physical form; this is so the spirit can evolve and attain perfection. For most spirits, this is their main purpose for being here on earth.

Plants are considered first density spirits, animals are second density spirits, and humans are third density spirits. When a spirit graduates from a second density to become a human in the third density, it will be mentally and emotionally slow. It's a new experience that it has to be able to grasp and understand. It has to learn how to be a human.[1]

****

From birth to the age of two, the ego develops eight discrete circuits. Each distinct circuit takes three months to develop and then it will lock-in or solidify. The behaviors seen in each interval match up with the responses seen in a child during that three-month cycle. At the age of two, these eight circuits travel together, en masse, up to the thalamus of the higher self, where they are unified to produce integrity in the child.[4] When a child at two years of age looks in a mirror and know for the first time that it's looking at itself and not another child, then it becomes a fully developed third-density human.

****

You must realize your position of authority over the ego who must obey your edicts. But that can never happen if the rational self doesn't realize that they possess that right and have that responsibility. The lack of knowledge of that reality is what creates bad parents. A parent has two years to establish their authority over a child, namely the developing ego, to show that the parent is the alpha leader that does not put up with bad behavior. However, make sure you achieve that position without physical, emotional, or mental punishment. All you need to do is tell a toddler when it misbehaves is, "I'm the boss, so you do what I tell you to do." It only needs to understand its place and who is in command, just as you would relate to your own ego.

50

****

At two, the higher self starts developing and needs to demonstrate that it's a self-determining person and needs to assert its right to its individuality. It needs to stand up for its place as a sovereign person. That is the reason for its rebellion during the 'terrible twos.' By this time, it's a little late to insist on your right to be a parent, as it takes a formidable amount of energy and strategies to fight against both a child's ego who thinks it's the boss and the higher self who wants to assert its independence.

This same rule applies when you acquire a dog. If you don't assert your authority and let the pet know that you're the pack leader, then it can turn into the pet from hell. Either you claim your command to rule over the dog, (or the ego before the age of two) or take the easy path and operate on autopilot; let the dog (or the ego) do what they want. You've shown them that you're not a leader. The result is that you've created a situation where disruptive, detrimental behaviors, like temper-tantrums, fear, and insecurities, can become extremely difficult to handle.

****

Love is the most powerful behavior in your arsenal of tools. The second most dominant tool is gratitude. Grateful people are happier, less depressed, less stressed, and more satisfied with their lives and social relationships. When you're grateful, you look for the good points in another. So, gratitude revokes the ego's judgmental criticism and observes the desirable qualities in a person which can eventually bring joy into your life. The individualism that strives to achieve a separation from others creates an exponential increase in depression.

You can train yourself to look for things for which you are grateful. Gratitude can help you find happiness in almost any situation because there is usually something for which you can be thankful. Being thankful for your mate, friends, family, children, acquaintances, and other people you meet is a social skill you develop to give you higher levels of happiness and lower levels of stress and depression. Gratefulness is a behavioral skill that puts you in charge of the self.

Grateful people sleep better because they have fewer adverse opinions and more positive feelings just before going to sleep. Gratitude has been said to have one of the strongest links with good mental health than any other character trait.[5]

Your attitude about life is one of the most useful tools to help you claim your command of the ego and the other selves. When you develop an outlook with the intention of creating an inner harmony, gratitude, acceptance of others, and humor, you make yourself an influential person that can rule the self, as it allows you to handle any social situation.

Humor promotes a creative playfulness that encourages social cohesion, cooperation, and even altruism.[6] The ego has an attitude of selfishness, and selfishness is serious stuff. To combat the ego's mean-spirited, petty attitudes, you look at life with a little humor. Since humor is an aspect of play, and playful emotions are contagious, then humor serves the function of dissolving social tension.

****

Awareness is the behavior skill which allows you to experience love and gratitude. Mindfulness helps you to put up a barrier to the ego's ability to be in your head, blocking the ego's adverse outlook and cynical attitude that creates stress, anger, fears, and insecurities. When you lose awareness, the ego takes command of the steering wheel and takes you for a ride as its passenger. Mindfulness puts you back behind the wheel and in charge.

Chapter 7

The higher self resides in the creative half of the right neocortex and is the playful child within you. The higher self is your creative, innovative problem solver; your creative artist who loves dancing and other creative forms of adult play that expresses its originality and innovative nature. Creativity is an essential aspect of play, humor, and personality. The higher self is your musical composer, your tactical general, your strategic chess player, who sees the 'forest' and patterns and thinks outside of the box when finding solutions to problems.

****

The growth of the ego occurs during the first two years of life. The higher self develops from two to five years of age. The four-year-old child is full of vitality and spontaneity and is referred to as an 'adult-child' because its personality is so similar to that of an adult.

The thalamus is the higher self's command center, located above the ego's hypothalamus. The thalamus has neural pathways to all aspects of the neocortical, gray matter of the right brain. The higher self operates below your awareness. Some refer to the higher self as your 'super conscience,' or the 'universal mind of God,' but those are references that apply to the 'soul,' not to the higher self.

Around the age of three or four, the higher self may develop an imaginary companion. This imaginary playmate is the ego. The higher self develops a relationship with the ego where it can act as the parent who guides and helps the ego. The higher self will generate a connection with the ego that is really like developing a friend. The higher self wants to learn how to establish relationships with other kids, but if there is a scarcity of kids around to interact and connect with, then an association with an alter-ego is more likely to occur, which can help achieve that need and intention.

****

The facial muscles are your domain, making you an actor that communicates the feelings of the higher self. Although the higher self has access and use of the facial muscles, you are the primary commander of the expressions of the facial muscles. You have the rational, judgment, perception, reasoning, and discernment to determine how the higher self's emotional feelings should best be expressed. Your communications of the higher self's emotional state represent your personality; so, the higher self and you are a coalition that reveals your personality.

An awareness of the higher self's emotions shows that you have an appreciation for its feelings. When you are conscience of your higher self's feelings, it's like showing gratefulness to your higher self.

The higher self reacts with appropriate emotions to different situations. Your expressions of the feelings that the higher self is experiencing is a creative act that can embellish life. The higher self responds to situations with feelings of what it's experiencing, and you express these sentiments with the facial muscles. Your personality is a team effort that communicates life's pleasures, problems, and stresses.

People who lack emotional expressions are inclined to anti-social behaviors which are a direct reflection of their mental health and suppressed emotions.[1]

Having an awareness of your facial muscles when you act or react helps put you in the 'moment.' This allows you to take charge of the mind and be the master of the self. This mindfulness of the facial muscles enhances your personality and gives you a 'presence.'

The higher self shows a consistent integration of the circuits of its brain that unites its various parts to create an attitude of integrity that, 'we are one!' By its nature, the higher self tends to produce a feeling of social connectivity, a sense of oneness, of tolerance, and of social equality.

During the development of the higher self at the age of four, healthy kids are altruistic by nature. They are open, approachable, and friendly to everyone, regardless of their looks or status.

An essential aspect of the higher self's nature is having integrity and being true to oneself. The higher self represents one's 'conscience.' Abuse of the higher self during the terrible twos is when the growth of a conscience can be hampered or impeded.

****

The higher self develops again during the middle school years, between the ages of 12 to 15 years. Schools are an example of how the Status social system can corrupt the higher self's true nature.

The higher self's integrity and belief in equality are subjugated in this Status oriented school setting. Status creates judgmental and critical discrimination that leads to intolerance and rejection. It is easy to find fault in the behavior of others and make it a recreational diversion. Some try to find shortcomings in others and talk about them behind their back, as a form of amusement. This criticism lowers the worth of the victim, while raising the social rank of respect for the abuser by making others feel intimidated by their capacity to use insinuation and innuendo to hurt others.

Social Status seekers judge and criticize others, looking for weaknesses that can be used against them to facilitate their advancement or popularity; and their own uncertainties may cause them to believe that they may also need to protect their esteem and respect from any attacks in the future.

Social Status has become so entrenched in the schools, that many school kids have found it to be a very unpleasant experience. Many former students remember their school years with painful memories. Bullying is a common occurrence, as one in three children are affected by bullying.

****

I believe the parent has to teach a child at an early age, between five-and-a-half and six years old, how important the skill of awareness is for growth and development. And we can make our youth more secure by providing them with knowledge about the ego.

So when a child is anxious, they may begin to avoid social interaction and associate many things with fear. This can be scary for the children because they don't necessarily understand why they act and think the way that they do. Recognized early, he or she can become acquainted and informed about the ego and the higher self and become more aware about what is happening. Thus, the child can incorporate this new behavior into its everyday life. This is opposed to adults who might not recover as quickly because it is more difficult for them to adapt.[2]

Kids would be better able to deal with bullies if we first inform them of the behavioral tools that control the ego. It's the ego that's intimidated by bullies! And it's the ego's imagination that magnifies the fear, because the child's conscious, rational self, cannot be scared. It's the ego that gets frightened; so, you can teach the child how to protect the ego by showing how to keep control

55

of the mind and the ego with the many skills of awareness, e.g. awareness of hand movements.

When a child discovers that he or she is the boss of the ego and begins to control the mind with awareness, then this child can become stronger than a bully; because he can now look a bully in the eye and let him know who the real head honcho is here. This kind of attitude gives the child a self-assertive feeling; whereas, bullies come from a state of comparative weakness because of the control the ego has over their mind which can create a relative state of emotional or mental weakness. Many people feel bullies underneath their bravado to be basically cowards. Anyone who tries to control another has a fragile frame of mind, because of the control the ego has over his or her emotional and mental state which can easily make him or her feel inadequate to handle situations when they encounter someone who has real self-control. This holds true also for women who are bullied by someone who is trying to control them.

We need to work together to cultivate and operate a flat, accepting environment in our schools instead of a rejecting, Status, ranking atmosphere that takes advantage of our students' need for acceptance and belonging. We can overcome the denigrating milieu created by Status by adopting a Synergic social ambiance that's conducive to learning.

****

The eyes are the domain of the higher self. When looking into someone's eyes, you are looking into the disposition of the higher self. The eyes express the emotional state of the higher self, whether sad, happy, inquisitive, perplexed, fearful, loving, indifferent, tired, etcetera.

From my experience, it is my belief that when the white part of the eyes occurs between the upper eyelids and the iris, the higher self will primarily be ruled by the motor nervous system, but there can be a secondary influence by an 'adventurous' ego with a strong motor system.

When the whites show up between the lower eyelids and the iris, then the higher self will be mostly influenced by the autonomic nervous system, but it is possible to have a bit of this effect by a 'merging' ego with a strong autonomic system.

When no whites appear, neither above nor below, then the sensory nervous system of the higher self will be most dominating, although the 'open' ego with a strong sensory system may also have some effect.

The eyes of the higher self may shift back and forth when it's overwhelmed with distress from the ego's drama or when the ego is upset with someone. A behavioral tool to give the higher self relief occurs when you stare with awareness, either unfocused or focused. A mindful stare helps the higher self relax and puts you in a calm altered state called the 'present.' When you stare with awareness, you can get an 'alpha' wave pattern where the brain cells fire together in harmony.

****

The ego may feel disrespected, insulted, excluded or rejected by some incident which then can be augmented by the ego's imagination where it can blow a situation entirely out of all proportions. This judgment turns into a belief, then a conviction that there is a lack of respect and a lack of acceptance of the self. The higher self can be overwhelmed by the ego's drama and eventually give in to a judgment coming from the ego and incorporate it as a belief that is demoralizing and depressive.

When both the higher self and the ego believe in a demoralizing belief, it can disintegrate into mutual feelings of hopelessness and despair; then a deep depression can occur because both the higher self and the ego have combined together to collapse into mutual feelings of hopelessness and despair. A deep sadness can eventually result in overwhelming unhappiness and misery in the isolation created by a Status culture.

Depression can change the whole dynamic of a relationship, and often is a deal breaker for a future together. Deep depression occurs when both the higher self and the ego unite together to collapse and disintegrate into mutual feelings of hopelessness and despair.

Depression endures because of a lack of understanding that it is your responsibility, the logical, rational self, to pull the higher self and the ego out of a depressive quagmire and return to a state of normalcy.

Depression can be overwhelming. It can create a sense of helplessness. But the worst thing you can do is give up and let the passage of time be a cure. By giving up, you have surrendered your authority and allowed the beliefs of the ego and the higher self to rule.

There's a good chance the higher self and the ego have developed an attitude that causes them to think they are not worthy, or inferior in some way. The ego and the higher self cannot continue to believe in such demeaning ideas about themselves. They are to obey your commands and your authority. They are not the captain of the ship. You are! They are to act in a way that coincides with your beliefs and behave in a manner that you deem is appropriate.

If you believe you are inadequate, unemployable, or unlovable, it doesn't mean it's correct. It's an illogical conclusion that the ego has converted into a belief because it constantly lives in your mind.

Beliefs become established because of the ego's control of the mind. We don't realize we have some of these beliefs or ideas unless we stop and analyze them. They can have consequences. There is a link between beliefs and adverse results. Examine negative beliefs and realize they originate from your ego.

You, the higher self, and the ego are not a democracy. You are the head director who rules. You do not argue with the ego or the higher self. You put your foot down and command them with statements that are expressed, silently and internally, "We are going to live in the moment; we are not going to live in the past, and we are not going to have fears about the future. You follow my beliefs as I decide what is important in our life."

****

You take back your command when depressed by using the facial muscles to express many different kinds of smiles. You regain your proper place as the commander-in-chief with exercises that employ various expressions of smiling. You cannot be depressed. You have no neural network to make that happen, but you can feel the torment and agony created by their depression. So, you are able to smile even though the ego and the higher self are suffering.

****

A repertoire of different types of smiles could be a smile with the corners of the mouth turned down, a smile showing your lower teeth, a smile showing your upper teeth, a smile showing both your upper and lower teeth together, smile with your cheeks, smile with your eyes while puckering your lips, smile while furrowing your brow, smile with an open mouth, etcetera.

Creating different types of smiles is an effort made by you to regain control of the mind and the body. Do not let the expression of a smile freeze or become rigid on your face. A smile should last five to ten-seconds, as you continue to express your repertoire of different smiles.

No matter how miserable or wretched you feel, remember these feelings are coming from the ego and the higher self and not from you; so, you are able to rise above their negativity by reestablishing your rightful authority by smiling. Even though you don't feel like it, you need to exert your power and dominance by smiling.

You make this extraordinary effort to assert your command of the self. Smiling tells both the ego and the higher self, "My attitude rules here; so, lighten up, and understand you are worthy and that your beliefs are wrong! You are to abide and follow my rules."

During bouts of depression, being able to express gratitude will serve to strengthen a positive experience about life. Even though you're sad, try to be thankful for what you have and for the people you know. You'll be surprised how this small change in your attitude can uplift your psyche.

You fight through the overwhelming hopelessness of depression, because the ego and the higher self are in control of the mind. The physical activity of smiling will let you regain control of the mind and allow you to rule the day as you overcome depression! Making use of the facial muscles by smiling regains control of the self.

Depending on how resolute you are, and how often you employ these smiling exercises, if you persist, it is the narrator's conviction that you can come out of a deep, severe depression within a day.

Shakespeare said, "You become the mask you wear!" You can transform both the ego and the high self away from feeling like a poor unfortunate, to a personality who is worthy and hopeful. When you reclaim your command, and know that the ego and the higher self are required to capitulate to your directions, then you become the true king of your kingdom.

When you don't make an effort and are depressed, then the brain activity will be low in the frontal neocortex. The solution is to make the effort to use the facial muscles as goal-directed tools to reactivate your frontal neocortex. This way your thoughts and beliefs can govern. The willpower to practice the smiling exercises allows you to rule and to put you back in control of the mind effectively.

****

People can achieve many things in life, like Anthony Bourdain, Kate Spade, or Robin Williams. They can attain the things they want in life and mysteriously commit suicide. This happens because they have no knowledge of this independent, separate entity called the ego. Brilliant people with will and effort can block out a lot of the ego's interference. However, the ego wants to be the boss, and unless told differently, will resent having that power taken away.

So remarkable people without the knowledge to keep the ego it in its proper place as an underling who is to serve the will of the conscience self, will just not be equipped to deal with this pesky, persistent, irritating nuisance.

The ego will take out its frustration on what it believes is an intrusion into its rightful domain, as the one who should be in charge, with continual disparagements, humiliations and criticisms, that can lead to low spirits, moods of sadness and depression that is difficult to battle and can lead to excessive drinking or psych pills. A person who has to make appearances every day in public, where it is important for them to appear upbeat and cheerful, can build-up a lot of psychological pressure that life can become more than he or she wants to handle.

Once they understand the power they have over this immature entity, they only have to let their ego know that it's only a servant who must carry out the intentions and will of the conscience self. This proclamation that they are the lord and master over the ego will immediately cause it to take it a back seat and act as a subordinate and follow your commands. Once you've told the ego that you are boss, the ego will accept your declaration and obey you, then you can tell the ego to stop all deflating, humiliations, criticisms and comments about the self, and the ego will follow your instruction.

When the ambiguities about who is the boss have been resolved, there is no longer any justification for the ego to be upset and angry. Then the drama and tragedy of the ego making disparaging remarks about the self and taking their own life can be eliminated. When the ego knows its place, it removes the source of the its anger. This stops the beliefs by the ego that it's in charge so it will not build up so much anger that can sit there and fester.

****

When the ego dominates with thoughts about the past or future, it's in charge, and you're going to have brain waves that have a random, irregular firing pattern with a high-frequency rate, which lacks harmony, called 'beta waves.' The irregular firing pattern of 'beta waves' is when the ego is at home, in its natural element. The ego's thoughts create a random, high-frequency firing pattern, and this is where the ego spends most of the day occupying your mind with 'beta waves' that enhances its ability to be in a hurry and thinking all the time.

The ego does not like the peace found in the 'alpha brain wave' state. It becomes a bystander, a spectator sitting on the sidelines. The ego wants to be part of the action; it wants to feel important; it thrives in the thinking, 'beta wave' brain pattern that produces drama, worry, regret, and stress.

The ego is excited and enthralled with a mob or a riot because it's running the show and in charge! When you're restless, irritable, impatient, bored, anxious, angry, in a hurry or resentful, the ego is in control. It creates stress by generating random 'beta' brain waves. This low-quality thinking pattern of the ego shows it has no aptitude to be in charge of the self and to be the boss.

****

To have a healthy relationship with another, you first need to have a healthy relationship with yourself. You do that by being responsible for the well-being of the higher self and the ego, and to look out for their welfare. You are the captain of the other selves, as you have the tools needed to protect the body, the ego, and the higher self from the stress and problems of life. Remember your most important behavioral tool is awareness! The second most important tool is to realize that you're the commander who the other-selves must obey.

Chapter 8

Once a neighbor, a friend, or a couple starts fighting, the ego takes over their minds by default. Scraps between couples often suffer from the loss of rationality and logic. The ego thrives on this drama because it gets the upper hand and assumes control. Arguing and fighting will not solve a problem. Kindness is the best solution for most difficulties.

After the initial novelty and enthusiasm of a new relationship, the ego will insidiously begin to undermine the intimacy of an emotional connection. The ego dislikes closeness because it weakens its control. After the initial period of enthusiasm, the ego will insidiously begin to encourage a reserve that can undermine closeness in a relationship. The ego has many tricks up its sleeve to subvert an amorous alliance. To be in an enduring and stable partnership, you need to have an arsenal of behavioral tools that will impede the ego's thoughts so that you have control of your mind that will put you in charge.

****

An action that's always at your beck and call is 'effort.' Making an effort increases your awareness. Willpower can give you the ability to be in control of the mind. If you want the easy life and kick back and operate on automatic pilot, then you've given up control and handed over the rule of the self to the ego. But if you strive and exert yourself, you increase your capacity to block out the ego's thoughts and stay in control.

A child who had parents that would frequently do everything for them, grew up without having to do anything for himself as a part of everyday life. The parent would cater to a child's every whim to produce an easy life without challenges and created feelings that they have rights of entitlements and claims on life that are not realistic.

It may be difficult for this child to learn to overcome difficulties from personal effort, which will help the person develop self-discipline. So, as adult, he or she will have a rough time of it, as his/her ego is going to have more of a say about who's in charge and dominate them more compared to others.

One cannot spoil a child by loving it too much. A child is spoiled when you do everything for it. When a child does not have to do anything for itself or does not have any responsibilities, then the parents are raising a child with an ego who is not only likely to misbehave because it believes it's the boss, but later in life, he or she is likely to be more troubled by the ego than others.

****

Awareness of your movements is a behavioral tool. When you use your hand to pick something up, to wash something, or cutting up food, be aware of the motions the hands are making. You don't want to think about what your hands are going to do because that occurs when you're in training to learn something new. But awareness of what your hands are doing is an entirely different classification or category than thinking about what your hands are doing. You do this to develop the skill of awareness.

Awareness is an exercise you have to practice, practice, practice, so that the effort becomes second nature to you, so it becomes a habit or becomes part of your belief system.

Be aware of using the thighs instead of the calves when walking; use the shoulders instead of swinging the arms. Try stretching out while walking or sitting instead of slumping or collapsing the body in on itself. Become aware of the things you do.

****

The left side of the body belongs to the ego while the right side belongs to you. If the left arm swings more than the right arm, it indicates the ego dominates and is in charge of the mind.

The ego can create a lot of stress on the left side of the body. The left side is where physical health problems often occur because of the emotional and psychic stress generated by the ego.

Based on observing the anger, fear, and insecurities operating within and among people, I would estimate that the ego controls 98% or more of the world's population. For example, if you were to watch people walk, almost all people swing their left arm more than they swing their right. It is rare to see one swinging the right arm more than the left because that would mean their rational, logical mind is in control. However, a closer look may reveal the person is left-handed, and the location of that ego is on the opposite side, or the person is in pain because pain forces you to be aware.

63

****

The ego usually dominates in the morning, and it has an agenda it wants to pursue. The ego will have us running around in a hurried manner, making us nervous and causing our movements to be rushed, which can result in mishaps or accidents.

The ego is our efficiency expert and wants to take short cuts. It intends to get through the busy things we have to do as fast as possible. We try to keep busy to avoid the ego's thoughts. But the ego has ideas it wants to convey and things it wants to do, which we have blocked with our busyness.

Like Alice's 'Mad Hatter,' the ego will try to hurry and rush our movements. When left unimpeded, the ego can leave us stressed, agitated, and exhausted. The behavioral tools of expanding the tongue, suspending our breathing, and awareness of our movement will allow us to relax and calm the ego.

Slow your movements down with smooth, creative, graceful motions of mindfulness. Moving with awareness creates smooth, flowing motions to make you mindful of what you're doing. Movements used with consciousness are like a creative dance. It's a responsive tool that slows you down and lets you stay in charge of your mind.

Dance with awareness to one of your favorite songs. Dance with meaningful movements, so your body smoothly flows and realizes an inner harmony. Keep your feet still to increase the awareness of how creatively your hips, shoulders, arms, and hands are moving. To reestablish the command of your mind, dance anytime you get a couple of minutes and do it because it's fun.

You practice dancing with mindfulness, and you practice moving your hands and body with awareness to raise your level of consciousness. You melt into the motions of your body to strengthen awareness and become the ruler of yourself.

****

When we get behind the wheel of a vehicle without awareness, we are handing over the keys of the car to the ego. The ego takes over the mind, and its inclination to be in a hurry can turn slight inconveniences into stressful feelings and impatience. Driving can then become very frustrating and irritating, causing you to be uneasy or nervous.

The ego wants to control other drivers and be a policeman; then be upset with them, when they don't do what it thinks they should do. When other cars are around, the ego's desire to control others causes a kind of mob mentality to develop. Often, driving turns into a battle between egos. When the light turns green, they mindlessly speed up to a red light a block away to slam on the brakes again.

Many people drive on automatic pilot; their lack of awareness makes them unconscious. Their minds leave the present and become involved in something that happened or will happen, causing them to be driving in an unsafe, vulnerable state. Driving becomes a stressful activity when you allow the ego to take over the steering wheel.

When mindlessly driving, lost in the ego's thoughts, people become susceptible to its adverse feelings of control that can make them irritable, upset, or angry. This emotional state generated by the ego's exasperation at those who are defying its unwritten rules of the road can get it so upset with those who are not behaving the way they should, that the ego can drag them down and leave them vulnerable to uncontrollable road rage.

If you drive with one hand, don't let the ego handle the car with its left hand, as the ego may overreact to a situation, for example, it may cause you to swerve off the road to avoid an animal that darts in front of the car. The ego will want to control the steering wheel, so you have to make a conscious effort to use the right hand.

****

When you've blocked the ego's thoughts and created a clear mind, then you can decide how you like to feel about life. Creating a state of mindfulness with an unobstructed mind, allows you to develop a positive attitude about life. This tabula rasa permits you to create an emotional milieu you choose to live with, like peacefulness, calmness, serenity, joy, love, gratitude, etcetera.

Whatever you decide and intend to create is the determinate factor in how you want to live your life! When you apply a feeling to your awareness, then the power of awareness is strengthened. As the commander of the self, you have the power to do this. This act of bringing awareness, feelings, and choice into driving can turn driving into something you could find pleasant.

****

Humming, singing, or whistling puts you in the 'moment.' Monks chant for hours at a time to keep them in control and 'present.' The adage of whistling in the dark when you're scared works, because the awareness of whistling lets you stay in the present and keep the ego's thoughts out of your head. You can't be scared when you're in the present unless there's a real threat to life and the 'body' becomes involved with a fight or flight response

****

Stutterers never stutter when singing, as they are in the present and awareness is operating to shutout the ego when they sing. Stuttering is caused by the ego's fears plus its impatience and hurried rush. The ego is scared that stuttering will reap ridicule and laughter, so it expresses an idea as fast as possible, which makes the stuttering worse. Stutterers can overcome the ego's angst that causes them to stutter by taking back the control of the mind, and not letting the ego invade their head with its hurried fears.

Overcoming stuttering begins with a soft stare and a knitted brow. Then expand the tongue, so it touches the roof of the mouth and extends slightly beyond the teeth. Next, stop breathing to increase your awareness. This action will help you to speak without stuttering because it requires a hyper-aware state that can block out the ego's thoughts.

When the ego is in control, it takes things too seriously. A stutterer should order the ego to lighten up, and needs to smile as much as possible as an example for the ego to follow.

****

The body is a learning device. Be aware of what goes on inside the body. Pain provides an awareness that puts you in the present. Perform a full body scan from head to foot. Try to be aware of any tension or discomfort in the body. Are the teeth and jaw clenched? Is there tightness around the stomach area? Is there any tension around the shoulders and neck area? You loosen up these areas by commanding the 'body' to relax those areas. You tell the 'body' to do that for you and it will de-stress those parts of the body for you.

Being aware of what's going on around you, puts you in the 'moment.' See the beauty everywhere. See the beauty in the sky and the clouds. Enjoy a sunset. Appreciate the magnificent beauty of trees and nature. See the beauty in man-made objects. Feel the wind against the skin. Stop and smell the roses and the coffee. Listen and be alert to the sounds around you, a cricket, a frog, the wind, the song of a bird.

Listen to what a person says instead of thinking what you want to say. Listening takes effort. If your attention starts to wander while listening to someone, the ego has taken over your thoughts. The ego is letting you know that its agenda is more important than yours. To listen to someone takes effort, when the ego intrudes with thoughts of what it wants to convey, the ego will block out the message that the speaker was trying to get across because of its thoughts. If you feel bored from listening, know that boredom comes from the ego; your ability to create awareness will counteract a tendency to be bored.

****

An important attribute of being a top-flight poker player in a high-stakes game is the ability to keep a poker face, so they don't betray their hand with a 'tell.' A 'tell' is a subconscious, involuntary facial or body reaction of the ego when a card appears that is surprisingly good or bad. The most successful players would have the ability to block out the ego's thoughts and stay in the present. They have learned how to be 'cool' with mindfulness and to be in control of the self in this type of situation. Anyone at the top of their game would have the behavioral tools of awareness that would allow them to stay in the 'zone.'

****

If we were to look closely at the low quality of the ego's thoughts, we would see how much of the ego's beliefs come through as minutiae about what has happened or what might happen. Without knowledge about the ego, we won't understand the disruptive behaviors we see in ourselves and others that create havoc and turmoil in relationships. The ego's impulse to be in control and apart from others is the reason and motive for the drama and disorder it creates.

Not knowing and not understanding the ego, we yield to the negative feelings coming from within, believing these gut feelings represent our essential self. Thus, we undermine our relationships with judgments, criticisms, disagreements, and arguments coming from the ego when we should be encouraging our partner in their endeavors and supporting each other with gratitude, love, and respect.

Chapter 9

You can control the chatter coming from the ego by meditating. When you meditate successfully, there are no thoughts in your head. Once an idea enters your head, the ego has invaded your mind, and you are no longer meditating. You have instead surrendered the 'present' to allow your ego to step in and occupy your head with its thoughts and its common concerns with everyday past events or worries of what might happen. This yammering is what the ego does all day long; it wants to be involved with the hustle and bustle of our daily activities. When the ego's thoughts disrupt your meditation, do not get upset, but instead focus on your breathing to stop the prattle, then continue with your meditation.

A method to do this is by chanting or by humming the sound 'ohm.' Mantras help you clear your mind of the clutter and busyness created by the ego. However, mantras are not very practical when carrying out your everyday activities and interactions. A 'guided meditation,' where you close your eyes and listen to a spoken message given to a group of people, has the same problem.

You can integrate meditation into ordinary daily activities when you do it on your own. The meditation you practice when you're alone is a more useful method of developing mindfulness. There are opportunities to meditate throughout the day. You can meditate when you are waiting in line, sitting for an appointment in an office, etc. You can meditate with alert awareness while driving. Meditation gives you command of the mind, and provides you a chance to practice, and develops your skills of awareness.

Meditation is a significant action, as its practice develops the skills of awareness and clears the mind for you to be in control. Meditation is a skill that takes intention, time, effort, self-discipline, and practice.

Awareness is all you need to be able to meditate. The first thing you want to do is see if there is any tension in your body. If there is, you tell or command the 'body' to relax that area and the 'body' will follow your direction and relax that area. Then pick out an object to engulf it with awareness.

When the eyes shift too rapidly, opportunities are created for the ego to slip into your head and regain control of your thoughts and mind. You control the eye movements when you stare with awareness.

Start your meditation by picking out something to concentrate on and engulf it with awareness. Create a 'feeling' that you want to cultivate. Peace and serenity are examples of emotions you may want to create in your life. Choose an object that has your interest. You may want to meditate for five or ten minutes; once the effort to be aware weakens, the ego is going to jump at the chance to enter the mind with its thoughts; so, you must recognize when this occurs and reset the clock and start again.

Starting over is not a failure, but a way to teach you how to meditate. The more you practice, the stronger your ability to meditate becomes. The more you meditate, the more your beliefs will be accepted, adopted, and believed by both the ego and the higher self. With enough practice, you may be able to meditate for an hour or more.

The ego hates it when you meditate. When the ego overwhelms you with some crisis filled with drama involving someone else, or won't let some matter rest, no matter what you try, then you can get the ego to give up the drama if you threaten to meditate for a significant amount of time.

When meditating and keeping your mind free of thoughts, you want to build on this clean slate of awareness; those feelings that you desire, like tranquility, serenity, or love. When you apply a feeling to your awareness, then your awareness is reinforced and fortified.

Your intention of creating inner peace and calmness will sprout a sense of well-being that can make daily activities more enjoyable. As you become conscious of this inner relaxing, flexible resilience, you start to lighten up and accept things as they are. You weaken your character when you express the ego's inflexible, severe, controlling beliefs.

You can integrate your personality into your mediation periods by employing your fascial muscles. You can practice the various methods of smiling, raising or furrowing the brow, etc.

****

The ego can be in your head continuously about some mistake you've made or some beef with a family member, a neighbor, or an acquaintance. The ego takes control over you because of the emotional drama involved with the upsetting event. You want to increase your awareness of as many things as possible to fight and overcome the ego's obsessive energy. Pick out an object or a painting to stare at, concentrate all your attention on it, and attach some feeling or emotion to it.

When you react with a response or an action to a compulsive thought coming from the ego, then you need to enhance your awareness to fight back against the ego's obsessive desire and regain control of the mind and the self. The more things you can be aware of in and around you, the stronger and more powerful your awareness will be. You need a reservoir of tools available to use with this type of meditation to combat the ego's stronger, obsessive-compulsive drive to be in control. These behavioral devices are especially important to those with OCD or phobias.

This overwhelming assault on your consciousness from the ego requires you to ramp up your awareness with a maximum effort. You do that by using all your senses. Be aware of what is happening within your peripheral vision; listen to the sounds around you or the sound of your breathing. Light a scented candle, spray some perfume, or open a bottle of vanilla extract to smell. Lightly stroke your skin or your hair to experience and be aware of the sense of touch. Listen to the breath while practicing shallow breathing and be mindful of anything going on within your body, like do you sense any tension in your neck, back, shoulders, gut, etcetera. Use the sense of taste by savoring a mint, a dab of peanut butter, a piece of hard candy, a whole clove of garlic to move around in your mouth but not bitten. Use your facial muscles to augment awareness, like furrowing or raising the brow, try different smiles, squint or blink the eyes, expand the tongue.

You can repeat silently "Tick, Tock" continuously, or repeat a mantra that will fulfill your intentions, like "I will love myself;" you cannot love others until you learn to love yourself. You can also repeat some motto that's appropriate for your goals of desires. This simple tool blocks the ego's access to your mind so that you occupy the mind instead of the ego.

Those with OCD, PTSD, or a phobia need a vast arsenal of tools because of the great control and mastery the ego has achieved over the rational self. If you have an OCD or a phobia, it means you're a captive of the ego, who has made you its prisoner. You have given up your authority and allowed the ego to take over the rule of the self. It is necessary for you to take these extraordinary measures and make a maximum effort to reclaim your control over the ego and regain your control of your mind.

When the ego continues to pound into your head some obsessive thought or repeatedly causes you to act in some compulsive manner, or when you feel overwhelmed, baffled, and hopelessly lost, then you need to use all your senses to strengthen your power of awareness. This type of meditation can be a powerful method to help you reclaim your rightful authority over the self in very emotionally disruptive conditions.

****

A mentally ill person, like a person with schizophrenia, has allowed the ego to take over almost all control of the mind. This person has no information on how his rational brain can reassert itself and regain command of the self. The individual does not know how to direct, use, and apply his will to control the ego and instead becomes hopelessly lost. Without knowledge of this inner, immature being called the ego, all his efforts seem to go for naught, to be of little use. He capitulates to this imaginary world that is a reality to the ego, so his mental existence becomes his physical life.

Devolvement into mental disorders occurs because of a lack of knowledge about the way the ego controls the mind and believes it is in charge of the self. When the ego rules the self without the behavioral tools of awareness to bar the ego's thoughts from the mind, then one doesn't stand much of a chance to overcome the struggle to free one's self from the grip of the ego and be in charge of the self. Especially, when there is no understanding of how the rational, conscious self is the real leader that controls the ego.

To be a success at what you want takes awareness, awareness, awareness; to be a ruler of the self you utilize that awareness with practice, practice, practice.

****

People in life or death circumstances, will take heroic actions and commit very courageous acts. They do things they normally would never be able to do.

Brave actions result because breathing will stop, senses become very sharp, and they become very alert. They become completely, 100% in the present. This awareness expels the ego from their consciousness to allow them to do some amazing things. When they are entirely engaged in an emergency, the ego is not allowed in the head, and there will be no uncertainty nor fear.

After the emergency is over, many will fall apart and start shaking uncontrollably as the ego regains its control of the mind. The person leaves the present and enters the ego's world of fear and 'what if' with all its other future imageries of what could have happened.

These heroic measures are a natural survival instinct that puts you in the present, so you can deal with a catastrophic emergency you normally wouldn't be able to handle because of the ego.

****

For you to 'think,' requires effort. For you to read a printed page demands the use of your will. When you relax that attempt, a sentence will need to be reread, as the ego will invade your mind with its thoughts, and you will not absorb or learn the words that were just read.

Humor, learning, planning, problem-solving, and creative ideas will originate from you and the higher self. These abilities grow when you learn to block the chaff and minutiae coming from the ego. Your potential will increase as you realize it is you, the rational and logical self, who decides and who is responsible for the well-being of your subjects, namely, the ego, the higher self, and the 'body.' An excellent tool to achieve these goals and become a master of the self is by practicing meditation.

Chapter 10

An important social factor involved in making friends and developing relationships is the expression of feelings with your personality. Showing your emotions with awareness allows you to convey a personal connection with someone you are interested in getting to know.

The facial muscles are primarily your domain. The emotions you perceive coming from the higher self are expressed by you with proper discernment. You express your beliefs sincerely and earnestly using your facial muscles with awareness! The higher self also has access to the facial muscles to communicate, if you are lethargic or lack energy.

Personality is a creative act and an important skill to help you rule the mind and gain mastery of yourself. Your expressions of the higher self's feelings are performances carried out by you. You communicate like an actor with 'presence,' on a stage of creativity.

All expressions of creativity put you in the 'moment' and block the ego's thoughts. Developing your personality is a never-ending, life-long endeavor. The personality you develop and the knowledge you acquire are the only things you can take with you from this life into your next life.[1]

Raising the brow reveals a sense of openness. Furrowing our brow with awareness help us to concentrate and reassures our command. This effort keeps us in the present; and because of an awareness of these fascial muscles, it keeps us in control of our mind.

Contracting the eye muscles with an intense, concentrated look can produce an energetic effect; or we can create a soft, seductive, alluring, gaze by relaxing the muscles around the eye. The cheek and eye muscles can be used to squint to aid concentration or to smile. We share the mouth muscles with the ego, and the movements and awareness of them keep us in the 'now' moment.

Awareness of the facial muscles allows you to block the ego's drama, so you're in control. The ego can take advantage of you when your energy is low and can quickly enter your mind. By activating the muscles of the face, you can pull out of a foggy state of mind. You switch on the facial muscles to reassert your authority. When your vitality ebbs, you can raise or furrow the brow. You can compress your facial muscles, squint or do any number of different facial expressions to retrieve ownership of the mind and get back to the present. When you use the facial muscles, it can be a helpful tool to enable you to take back command of the mind.

****

The ego can make you feel uncomfortable, embarrassed, awkward, or tense in a social situation. You can take back control of this situation by suspending your breath, staring with awareness, enlarging the tongue, and using the facial muscles to smile.

One of the most powerful behavioral tool or skill to accomplish this intention is by expressing a sense of gratitude for those around you. These techniques can relax the ego and the higher self, to promote a kind of casualness to help you and others to be more at ease.

A social encounter can feel tense when there is not some sense of gratitude evident. When you develop the attitude of being thankful for an acquaintance you just met, grateful for your friends, and appreciative of the situation you are in, then this inclination towards grace creates a relaxing and amiable connection with others or another.

People love pets because they are usually very gracious or thankful just to be in your presence; as a result, a pet can make almost anyone happy and relaxed to be around. Grateful people are happier, less depressed, less stressed, and more satisfied with their lives and social relationships.[2] Gratefulness is a social skill that enhances awareness. Showing appreciation towards others can put you in a good mood and make you lighthearted.

****

Displaying a sense of love can block the ego's angst or critical judgments and allow us to have a more rewarding or gratifying experience with another. Socially connecting with others is more relaxing and pleasant when we experience feelings of love which will restrict the ego's anxious thoughts. We become a master of love when we intentionally desire to be loving, and when we practice and act at being loving.

When personal problems occur, it's often caused by a lack of graciousness or a lack of love in our thinking. The ego would never allow such expressions of love and solicitude to occur as long as it's in control of your mind. Those who are greatly influenced by the ego will tend to have a disdain for love.

When we are in command of the mind without the ego's intrusions, we can bathe in the calm, peaceful pleasure of 'now.' You'll discover that this represents your real self. Your genuine self will be a state where you can feel calm and tranquility; when we reveal our authentic selves, we find peace with others.

****

Self-consciousness is a misnomer because the negative feelings it points out like being embarrassed, turning red, or blushing is a result of a lack of self-consciousness. Only by being aware of our facial expressions can we avoid these awkward stresses of self-consciousness.

When you use the facial muscles with no awareness of what the muscles of your face are doing, then you have invited the ego into your conscious mind and allowed it to rule with all of its drama and turmoil. When there is no mindfulness of what the facial muscles are doing, then the ego will be in charge and make you vulnerable to blushing.

Bringing forward our attention to what our facial muscles are doing will block out the ego's thoughts and concerns. Awareness of our expressions is the behavioral devise we use to help prevent blushing by keeping the ego out of our heads. Being conscious of our facial muscles is one method and tool available to us to enhance and evolve our strength of character.

****

Children need to be acquainted with the ego not only to develop their personality but to increase their good judgment, education, and intellectual capacity. A child should know how much influence and know how much control the ego exerts, know about the skills of awareness, know about his or her authority over the ego, and know his or her responsibilities for the other three selves.

When there is no familiarity with the ego, then it's difficult to navigate around the low quality, obsessive thoughts coming into the head from the ego and be aware that there are alternative options than those of the ego. The intellectual, low-level of opinions coming from the ego hinders their ability to develop both the rational and the problem-solving areas of their mind that are involved with schooling and involved with many areas of life.

****

The behavioral tools needed to control the ego are both awareness and effort. Effort is challenging and is not natural for us, but it is especially a 'pain' to youngsters. However, the rewards from employing our 'will' and using our awareness are going to pay off in a better and more enjoyable life. We all must strive and make an effort to develop the tools needed to deal with anxiety, fear, anger, and insecurities, in other words, the skills of awareness that allow us to cope with the ego.

The low-level of thoughts coming from the ego hinders our youth's ability to develop both the rational and the problem-solving areas involved with their schooling. This lack of guidance about the ego can affect their IQ score. When the mind is interrupted by the ego's lowly thoughts, then the ability to solve problems and to think logically and rationality have been encroached upon, so that they have been unduly influenced by the ego.

Most kids will, unfortunately, follow the easy path and let the ego think for them, and let it make decisions for them. Children can grow and mature emotionally and intellectually with both effort and knowledge about the ego.

A lack of knowledge about the ego will limit their capacity to choose a path in life that is more suitable to their nature and makeup. We can educate our children and empower them with the tools they need to deal with the ego and take control of their mind. This information expands their potential and enables them to make healthier choices and to flourish.

The higher self's creativity and problem-solving abilities, along with your logic and rationality, are brought together to create a team that helps you to block the ego from the mind and enables you to accomplish your goals. This intelligence is available to you when you restrict the ego's thoughts by using your skills of awareness. When we master these, we will have the powers to rule the self and overcome our fears, anger, and insecurities.

Chapter 11

The first lesson a Buddhist master will teach their students is how to breathe correctly before any other lesson can begin. We breathe every few seconds of our lives. We rarely go more than a minute without breathing. Some are unable to hold the breath without struggle and discomfort. Learning the proper breathing technique is one of the most important things we can do for our psychological, physical, mental, and spiritual well-being.

Your body requires a certain level of carbon dioxide in the lungs and bloodstream for it to operate properly, and to avoid health problems. When you breathe too fast, then you reduce the carbon dioxide level, and then your body reacts by locking up the available oxygen in the blood cells of the blood vessels.[1] This over-breathing is caused by the ego, because it desires excitement and drama, or because it feels stressed-out.

Taking deep breaths using the diaphragm has been mistakenly taught as the proper way to breathe. Breathing in this manner leads to our over-breathing that is detrimental to our health. The diaphragm should only be used to take deep breaths when we are physically active; even then, most people will rapidly pant causing the detrimental effects of over-breathing, instead of pausing after inhaling to a count of two to six.

Many people are over-breathers and are unaware that they are over-breathing. When we allow our ego to control our thinking, we lose awareness of how we are breathing. Inhaling and exhaling with a normal breath should take about five-seconds. Shorter breathing cycles mean you are over-breathing.

Anxiety, fear, anger, insecurities, confusion, stress, and excitement, and ill health are emotional conditions that the ego creates to cause you to breathe rapidly. The ego's drama operates in concert with its fast breathing without your knowledge to render you unconscious about how hurried your breathing has become. A lack of awareness allows the ego's cravings for excitement to dominate and make you over-breathe.

The proper way to breathe is to slow the breath down, so it takes five seconds to inhale, five seconds to suspend or hold the breath, and five seconds or more to exhale. Try to extend each breath. More oxygen is absorbed into the tissues of the body when we slow our breathing. It oxygenates our body and makes us healthier. Over-breathing creates a deficiency of oxygen to enable toxins and pathogens to start being established and grow.[2]

The problem with over-breathing or rapid breathing is exhaling. How we inhale is not a problem, because the amount of oxygen entering the red blood cells from the lungs, is constant at about a 98% uptake rate.

The trouble is, once the amount of carbon dioxide in the lungs falls below about 7%, the body reacts by locking up oxygen in the red blood cells because we exhaled too much carbon dioxide from breathing too fast. All of the hemoglobin within a red blood cell starts to lock up oxygen and won't release it back into the bloodstream. Then the oxygen can no longer move out of the red blood cells back into the areas where it is needed, namely into the cells or tissues of the body.[3,4.]

****

ATP is the energy system for the cells. If there were a lack of ATP in the body, death would come within fifteen seconds! The fuel that ATP needs is a mixture of oxygen and carbon dioxide. 100% pure oxygen is deadly. Just as the fuel for a car needs a combination of oxygen and hydrocarbons (gas), your body's ATP needs oxygen mixed with carbon dioxide. Keeping a reservoir of carbon dioxide in the lungs is imperative.

When the body's cells start to hunger for oxygen, you will experience a shortness of breath or air hunger, it's not oxygen your body hungers for and needs, but it's your body's hunger for carbon dioxide. If you start to pant or breathe deeper and faster, it will increase your air hunger, as it evacuates even more carbon dioxide from the lungs, which then causes the hemoglobin to lock up even more oxygen, till it seems like you're suffocating, and you can't catch your breath. It's not from a lack of oxygen that you're out of breath, but from a lack of carbon dioxide, because you've allowed the ego to dominate you and make you over-breathe.

Here we have oxygen-rich blood cells circulating throughout all the blood vessels of the body, while the body's cells or tissues are crying out desperately for oxygen that is locked up in red blood cells. That is why hyperventilating can cause a person to faint, because the brain was deprived of oxygen, and because the lungs and therefore the body's cells and tissues were denied the proper mixture of oxygen and carbon dioxide.

Nearly all cancer begins due to lack of cell oxygenation. Cancer attacks every organ in the body, except the heart, which uses an abnormally abundant supply of oxygen. When the body's cells are lacking oxygen, it can do a lot of damage to the body, as there are over twenty-one health problems attributed to the lack of oxygen.

Tens of thousands were cured of asthma by teaching and training them how to stop over-breathing in New Zealand, U.K., and Russia studies. (See www.sleepingallnight.com and www.buteyko.com.au)

When those with asthma become short of breath, they mistakenly start to breathe too quickly and over-breathe by gasping for air. When asthmatics start panting, they expel more and more carbon dioxide. Huffing and puffing cause the hemoglobin within the red blood cells to start locking up more and more oxygen.

A vicious cycle begins where they can spiral down, turn blue, lose consciousness, and even die, because they are unable to slow down their breathing to keep carbon dioxide in their lungs. As a result, over 5,000 people die from asthma each year, because they didn't understand how over-breathing can kill them.

This paradoxical situation, where iron-rich red blood cells, chock full of oxygen, are circulating throughout the body's blood vessels, while the cells of the body are crying out desperately for oxygen, which resulted from the low level of carbon dioxide in the lungs, because of rapid breathing, is known as the Bohr effect in the medical literature.[1,2,3,4.]

****

The body's natural defense to keep carbon dioxide in the lungs is to: 1. Narrow the airways with spasms. 2. Narrow the airways by developing mucus and phlegm. 3. Narrow the airways by swelling the mucous lining and the bronchial tubes.

Nature restricts the airways and creates these negative and often painful effects to keep carbon dioxide in the lungs. The pain and discomfort the body experiences is nature's alarm system warning you; you are doing something wrong! Namely, you are breathing too rapidly. You need to take over command of the ego and the 'body' and order them to start slowing down their breathing rate! But you are the responsible one who must set the example with a slower breathing rate.

Oxygen withheld from the cells of the body is going to create an unhealthy, anaerobic, acidic condition. Almost all toxic waste in the body is acid. The body eliminates acidic waste by vomiting and diarrhea, by coming out in skin eruptions, or by storing the toxins in fat cells.

Another way the body eliminates acidic waste is with an oxygen element. An oxygen element has to be available to chaperone an acidic toxin out of the body. So, when the body is not oxygenated, there is a buildup of toxins in the body which starts the disease process!

Acidosis is the real cause of asthmatics deaths. They turn blue before they die. But their death can be prevented by drinking a bottle of Pepto Bismol, or by drinking three teaspoons of sodium bicarbonate in a glass of water; this returns them to a more alkaline state and allows them to survive. When we over-breathe, we create a very unhealthy, acidic state in the body.

****

All headaches and migraines are caused by over-breathing. By learning how to stop over-breathing, we can prevent headaches and migraines. The brain is starved of oxygen when the ego over-breathes and locks up more and more oxygen. The brain's blood vessels start to expand and dilate to move oxygen into the cells of the brain. Dilated blood vessels are the only cause of pain in the brain.

But the problem is, the oxygen in the dilated blood vessels of the brain is locked-up in the red blood cells and can't be released for the brain to use. The oxygen is locked up by the hemoglobin within the red blood cells, because of the low carbon dioxide levels in the lungs, which were created by the ego's over-breathing.

****

People can get rid of a headache or a migraine within two minutes by holding their breath! You can hold your breath by filling the lungs with air and tighten the stomach muscles by 'bearing down.' Practice holding your breath, till you can get up to a count of 40, as a technique to control the mind. Those unable to do this, because of the ego's dominance can inhale to a slow count of six or eight, then exhale to a higher number. It can take up to five or six minutes to get rid of a migraine with slow breathing. The longer the time between breaths, the sooner a headache or a migraine will disappear!

If you're in severe pain from a headache or a migraine, cut off the zip lock end of a gallon plastic bag. Next, form a funnel with the bag using both hands so that the bag can fit under your chin and over your nose with a tight air seal, then breathe into the bag until the pain goes away.

Suspending the breath lets the carbon dioxide levels in the lungs build back up, so the hemoglobin will start releasing oxygen from the red blood cells to enter the oxygen-starved brain cells, and cause the red blood vessels in the brain to shrink down to its normal size and stop the pain.

Soon the headache will go away! You should never have to suffer from headaches or migraines for more than a few minutes ever again! Holding your breath will end all headaches, whether they are from a hangover, behind the eye, sinus, perfume allergy, tension, cluster, etc.

Experiencing air hunger while at rest, because you were using the diaphragm to take deep breaths which expelled too much carbon dioxide, starves the body of oxygen and causes nervousness, anxiety, chest pains, vertigo, cramps, shaking hands, chronic sinus problems, viral illness, and all the old age diseases.

We tend to over-breathe also because of physical illness, lack of sleep, and over sleeping. Any over-breathing during these times will make these conditions, discomforts, and pain worse.

****

The ego thinks and dreams at night about the events of the day. Most of the dreams people experience are expressions of how their ego feels. It lives in these fantasy worlds as if they were an actual reality. Unpleasant dreams can stress out the ego and make it upset, and the ego will often blame you for the suffering it experienced in the dreams.

Waking up in the morning, some may wonder why they're in such a sorry, quick-tempered, negative state. Why they feel so tired? Moody feelings result because the reality of the ego dreams was about things that were distressing the day before and it is upset because of these troubling situations. Dreams are a real event to the ego, and it may even be upset with you, because of your reactions or your inactions. Those feelings represent the ego's state of being during the night. Many need a cup of coffee in the morning to revive their vitality to be on an equal energy footing with their ego, and to restore their humor to overcome the negative mood that's upsetting the ego.

****

The daytime habits of over-breathing continue to occur in nighttime activity of dreaming. The practice of over-breathing during the day can be overcome and corrected by your conscience awareness. But when this habit of over-breathing carries over into your nighttime sleeping and dreaming

81

patterns, then there is no awareness that would allow you to correct this threatening condition. There is no conscious way of slowing down your breathing to stop the hemoglobin in the red blood cells from siphoning off all the oxygen in your bloodstream. This over-breathing at night is the reason so many people die in the middle of the night while they are asleep.

However, nature is cognizance of the direr, threatening conditions you are in and will stop breathing up to five minutes to allow the hemoglobin to release oxygen back into the bloodstream which will restore the body to a more balanced, alkaline state.

When you stop breathing during sleep, it will revitalize the body that was in trouble from over-breathing and removes the acidic waste so that you can stay alive. It's nature's way of saving your life and prevent a possible death that happens so often at night from the habit of daytime over-breathing.

****

The proper way to breathe is to take shallow breaths. Shallow breathing uses the chest and shoulder muscles to create a reservoir of carbon dioxide in the lower part of the lungs to help maintain a healthy level of carbon dioxide. Inhale to a count of five, hold the breath for a count of five, then exhale by relaxing the chest muscles. After inhaling, you can also exhale by letting the air out slowly in a relaxed way, like letting air out of a tire.

Inhale with a large shallow breath, then ease the breath out as slowly as you can. As the breath leisurely escapes, create a pleasurable feeling or joy within you as the air is leaving your body. You can do this to help you fall asleep. A lack of sleep can become a routine that creates a pattern that produces the stress of anticipating insomnia, so you avoid going to bed and stay up late. Poor sleep can be improved when the ventral striatum, a reward center in the brain associated with optimism, is activated. Thus, pleasure can buffer the effect of poor sleep and feelings of joy can help you cope with a lack of sleep.[4]

Shallow breathing chest muscles are probably weak from disuse; you develop them by tensing your stomach muscles by 'bearing down' while expanding the chest and raising the shoulders. Employing the muscles that surround the diaphragm enables you to efficiently use the muscles involved in shallow breathing.

****

The 'body' is an independent entity with convictions it believes are best for the physical self. The 'body' resides within the hypothalamus of the left limbic brain and functions at an unconscious level. The 'body' develops from five to seven years of age, from fifteen to seventeen years, twenty-five to twenty-seven years, and thirty-five to thirty-seven years.

The 'body' is subordinate to you and must obey you whenever it can. You can tell the 'body' to shallow-breathe, and the 'body' will do that for you. But the custom of deep breathing with the diaphragm is a routine it's been practicing its whole life. The 'body' has a lot of inertia, so it is easy for it to slip back into its old habits. It can take a little persistence to remind the 'body' to shallow-breathe.

Being aware and engaging in shallow breathing is a practice we can use when meditating. Awareness of shallow breathing during meditation blocks the ego's thoughts from entering our head. Shallow breathing is an important activity that can improve our health, as it gradually shifts our body over into the alkaline pH side and oxygenates the body.

Health problems can compromise your immune system. You should shallow-breathe to reduce the unbalanced acidic state to one that is more alkaline and to improve your chances of being healthy.

When you stop breathing or hold your breath, it is very healthy for you. It relaxes and calms the ego to provide a more amendable, personal connection with another, so it's important to understand the significance of slowing down the breathing rate in relationships. This behavioral skill of suspending the breath allows you to develop a relaxed, enjoyable, and loving relationship with someone important to you while improving your health.

Part Two

Chapter 12

The ego will often desire to be independent from others. The neural network and pathways of the ego's limbic brain show that the circuits of each of the eight growth periods are unconnected, discrete, and separated. This lack of integration that makes each circuit distinct is a significant influence that causes the ego to want to be separate, independent, and apart from others.

The ego grows from birth to two years of age. The ego develops again from ten to twelve years of age, from twenty to twenty-two years of age, and finally from thirty to thirty-two years of age. During the first two years of life, there are eight discrete, neural circuits and each of these eight distinct circuits produces actions which match the behaviors expected from those neural networks.

These eight discrete growth phases correlate with behaviors expected from those neural pathways, but have no integrating, neural pathways that would unite these different growth periods, circuits, and behaviors together. By its very physical construction, the ego will want to be separate from others.

****

You, the rational, conscious one, have growth periods that occur from 7 to 10 years of age. Your developmental phase occurs again from 17 to 20 years of age, from 27 to 30, and your final peak of growth occurs from 37 to 40 years of age. Some may have experienced how responsible a nine-year-old can be and even allow them to be a babysitter, but the eleven-year-old when the ego is developing, suddenly seems to have lost that sensibility and reliability and can no longer be trusted with too many responsibilities.

****

The 'body' resides within the hypothalamus of the left limbic brain and functions at an unconscious level. The 'body' will obey the instructions that come from you, the conscious self, and will also be influenced by the ego when it is in charge of the self.

The body's inertia causes it to avoid change. The 'body' will make itself known to you in a situation where your survival is at stake, when you experience an alarming 'fight or flight' reaction.

****

The growth of the ego occurs during the first three months of life and will develop an inertia type 'relaxation,' 'sleep,' or 'synchronal' response. It runs on a continuum from a state of relaxation to deep sleep. The 'vegetative' response influences oral activity, like sucking and feeding around the region of the mouth and a 'synchronal' response to produce rhythmical breathing and a relaxed tongue, and jaw. So, the ego has the ability to relax and sleep. When you feel uptight, you tell the ego to relax and it will try to do that for you.

Chapter 13

The 'synchronal,' 'relaxation,' or 'sleep' circuit evolves during the ego's first three months of development. These neural pathways, involving axons and neurons, are locked in at the end of the three-month growth period. These seem to lay down the major 'highways' of the brain's neural pathways, although smaller 'country roads' and 'byways' can always be developed later.[1,2,3.]

The 'synchronal' circuit, as shown in Fig. 1, refers to the medial preoptic, anterior, and posterior hypothalamus, olfactory bulb, medial and lateral olfactory stria, olfactory tubercle and gyrus, and anterior perforated substance regions. These areas are grouped together to represent the 'synchronal,' or sleep region, where 'vegetative,' responsive behaviors originate.

The anterior hypothalamus is the control center for the parasympathetic nervous system.[4,5.] Olfactory stimulation produces parasympathetic nervous system reactions, such as active intestinal peristalsis, increased gastric motility, hair-erection, salivation, urination, and defecation. It stops spontaneous movements by impairing consciousness with tired or sleepy feelings.[6]

The olfactory region has neural pathways to the neocortex, even in animals with no smell function such as dolphins. The olfactory region also has an emotional function that acts on the viscera to influence physical attitudes, disposition, and affective moods, by producing approach and avoidance reactions.[7]

The anterior and posterior hypothalamus influence approach and avoidance behaviors related to oral activities, such as sucking and feeding, along with the olfactory function of discriminating desirable from noxious odors that effect approach and avoidance responses.[8]

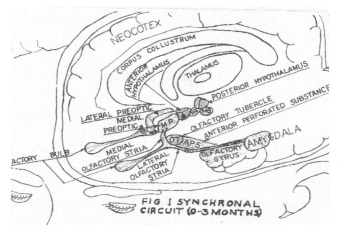

Fig 1. Synchronal Circuit (0–3 Months)

The preoptic area and anterior hypothalamus synchronize alpha and theta brain waves. The preoptic area is the sleep center at a higher level of functioning and control. When the preoptic area was destroyed, animals were not able to sleep.[9,10.]

Stimulation of the preoptic region can produce urination, defecation, and sleep, and can create synchronized alpha brain wave patterns that produce inactivity, lassitude, and drowsiness.[11,12,13,14,15,16.]

The preoptic area can terminate appetite by inhibiting desires for food, experienced as satiety to create a feeling of fullness. The preoptic area does this by changing the beta waves pattern that stimulates the appetite to slow synchronizing, theta brain wave rhythms.[17.]

People need to get eight hours of sleep. Those who suffer from insomnia or for those who have trouble sleeping, it seems to indicate that they have an ego that has forgotten or lost the ability to readily or adeptly perform the 'relaxation' or 'sleep' response.

A key to rediscover or relearn the 'relaxation, sleep' response is to practice a breathing habit or pattern that has a regular rhythm. It's best to find your own natural, rhythmical, breathing rate. If that's a problem, then try breathing as slow as possible with breaths that are as short as possible while still maintaining a constant rhythm by expanding the chest muscles.

To relearn the 'relaxation, sleep' response you want to relax the mouth and throat area by swelling or expanding the tongue with a slack jaw, and you want a mindless, unfocused stare.

Chapter 14

In the second three-month growth stage, from four through six months, the ego develops an 'approach' response. This area of the brain is a particularly strong pleasure area. Although there are pleasure areas in the 'vegetative' area of the brain, they are not nearly as strong.

The 'approach' and 'vegetative' responses combine to find great pleasure in sustenance. They are an aspect of the autonomic nervous system. Now, there develops an approach or looking to pleasure, as a good baby coos, smiles, or laughs easily.

The ability to relax during the first three-month period with the 'vegetative' response provides an important behavior to reduce stress. The 'approach' response during this second three-month period provides a positive social outlook on life. It influences an orientation towards pleasure.

Chapter 15

The 'approach' circuit refers to the corticomedial amygdala and the lateral olfactory stria and stria terminalis pathways with connections to the medial preoptic region and the anterior hypothalamus. The corticomedial amygdala has been found to be a particularly strong pleasure and reward center in electrical stimulation studies.[1,2,3,4.] These feelings are very similar to the emotional pleasure experienced in eating, especially when hungry. See Fig. 2.

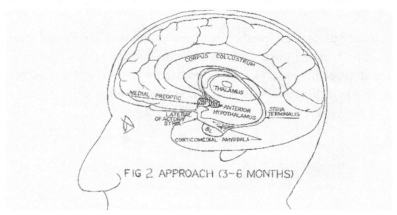

Fig 2. Approach (3–6 Months)

Chapter 16

In the third growth stage of the ego, during the seventh, eighth, and ninth months, there develops an 'avoidance' response that creates a searching, expectant attitude of anticipation.

The desire to avoid punishment has the power to motivate many times greater than the wish to approach pleasure. The 'avoidance' response guides one away from harm. It operates as a rapid alarm system to be alert when danger threatens. It's an aspect of the sensory nervous system.

****

A seven-month-old infant now shows a fearful reaction to what is unknown or unfamiliar as it can seem like a threat.[1]

The 'avoidance' response arouses defensive reactions for self-preservation.[2,3] The 'avoidance' area selects the right responses needed to get what is wanted or avoid irrelevant responses that aren't adaptive.[4]

In the seven-month-old, an object's novelty, uncertainty, or complexity may evoke a surprise response until the baby establishes some familiarity with it.[5]

The baby can now be easily aroused and stimulated so that he can play contentedly by himself needing little to keep him entertained. With this spontaneous self-activity, the baby is becoming self-contained and often happier alone.

The baby is beginning to realize some autonomy, as he develops an ability to differentiate individuals. He starts to narrow his interests to selected people familiar to him. This newly acquired ability to discriminate also makes the infant afraid of strangers.[6]

Separation anxiety, an aspect of self-preservation, also develops now.[7] If emotional attachments are not established by the infant during the last 'approach' period, before fear grows during this 'avoidance' phase, then the child will possibly not be ready again to develop positive emotional relationships with others until three years of age.[8]

Chapter 17

The ventral amygdalofugal and pallido hypothalamic fascicle nerve pathways represent the 'avoidance' circuit area. See figure 3.

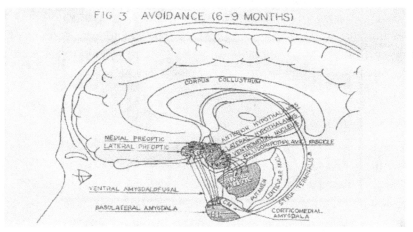

Fig 3. Avoidance (6–9 Months)

There is a lot of sensory information flowing into the basolateral amygdala from touch, sound, and visual stimulation, while little sensory data flows into the cortico-medial amygdala shown in the last approach period.

The globus pallidus, along with the ventromedial nucleus area of the hypothalamus, is developing the motor aspects of the 'avoidance' circuit.[1]

The basolateral amygdala aspect of the limbic nervous system has an irregular, rapid beta rhythm of 40–45 cycles per second when offensive stimuli is present.[2]

The basolateral area is connected with the pituitary-adrenal area to create a rapid alarm system, especially with Adrenocorticotropic hormone (ACTH) secretions.[3,4,5.]

Stimulation of the basolateral area creates inhibition of all on-going activity and orients the movements of the eyes and head in a searching response, creating an expectant attitude of attention.[6]

This basolateral response is similar to a curiosity response, where an object's uncertainty may evoke a surprise response in the seven-month-old and hold his attention until he is used to it. More intense stimulation of the basolateral amygdala gives rise to fear and defensive responses.[7]

The 'avoidance' circuit enhances the ability for one to be relevant. It determines appropriate responses to rewards and punishments,[8] and it regulates the role the basolateral plays in discrimination and generalization.[9,10]

The ability to discriminate creates a fear of strangers.[11] In self-stimulation studies, the basolateral area was found to be a punishing area of displeasure.[12,13]

Displeasure experienced from this area was feelings of hunger, thirst, choking, suffocation, nausea, gagging, retching, and the desire to defecate or urinate.

Some secondary effects were feelings of foreboding, fear, terror, paranoia, sadness, wanting to be alone, strangeness, and unreality.[14]

****

Both divisions of the amygdala function as a self-preservation mechanism. The amygdala has duel positive and negative functions. On the positive side in the cortical amygdala, it serves as an 'approach' response during the second three-month growth period, as it sets up social abilities with approach behavior, which can make self-preservation more successful in group situations and provides a positive social outlook on life and influences an orientation towards pleasure. Although the negative half in the basolateral side of the amygdala gives the ego the ability to discriminate along with the capacity to display some discernment, it also causes the anxious and fear responses of the avoidance or escape reactions.

The corticomedial amygdala is comparatively much smaller than the basolateral amygdala in cats with a dominant sensory nervous system, but these two divisions are equal in rats.[15,16] These nuclei show how important these areas are regarding the differences in behavior and temperament observed in these animals.

Thus, it can be extrapolated that the 'open' ego with a dominant sensory nervous system will have a corticomedial amygdala that is smaller than its basolateral amygdala. The 'merging' ego with a dominant autonomic nervous system would have these two divisions equal to each other. Or the corticomedial could even be larger in the 'merging' ego to give some explanation of the difference in behavior seen in these two types of egos.

Removing the amygdala caused humans to lose the ability to shift attention and to respond emotionally. They became inert, with less zest and intensity of emotions, and were less capable of creative productivity.[17.]

Chapter 18

The next three-month growth period, from the tenth through the twelfth months, sees the ego develop a 'discriminative' response. The child discriminates by avoiding that which is threatening, processing that which is significant and selectively screening out unnecessary information.

'The ten-month-old infant has learned to inhibit some of his impatience and wait for his meal. He concentrates when inspecting his toys; and his play shows more discrimination, as he may pretend to drink with a cup.

He recognizes when an object is missing. More demanding and insistent, he is beginning to show a temper. He is becoming socially discriminating and more sensitive to events in his environment. He responds more to demonstration and teaching, as he imitates others, and learns social types of games by playing pat-a-cake, bye-bye, and peek-a-boo.[1]*'*

Chapter 19

The 'discriminative' circuit, in Figure 4, consists primarily of the caudate nucleus with various connections to the hypothalamus, thalamus, globus pallidus, and putamen.

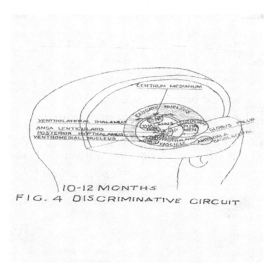

Fig 4. Discriminative Circuit (10–12 Months)

The caudate nucleus has reciprocal connections with the basolateral amygdala and the suppressor areas of the neocortex to influence an increased control over excitation, as its motor neurons operate to reduce sensory excitation when stimulated.[1,2,3]

The caudate nucleus provides the ability to process relevant information and selectively suppress that which is superfluous. This permits selective sensitivity that can heighten responsiveness to some specific interests, while reducing sensitivity to areas outside of those interests.

The caudate nucleus not only inhibits but has an excitatory aspect that can increase the curiosity derived from the basolateral amygdala to produce a very active exploratory drive.[4]

Chapter 20

The 'affective' response develops from one year of age to fifteen months. The 'affective' response is concerned with emotional responses involved with a sophisticated motor control of the autonomic (visceral) nervous system.

The ego's emotional ability to make better judgments improves, such as the decision to like or dislike something or to use the motor system to approach something or avoid something.

'*The one-year-old has increased social needs and is starting to enjoy the social give-and-take of play with adults. Because of the social reciprocity involved, the one-year-old sometimes becomes a surprisingly good imitator, as he intently watches facial expressions.*

He likes an audience, and to be the center of attention. He enjoys applause, and when he gets laughter from people from something he does, he will repeat the performance. The one-year-old engages in vigorous muscular activity and is starting to get into everything. He is very active and likes to play with several objects rather than one.[1.]

Chapter 21

The 'affective' circuit includes the cingulate area with pathways projecting from the mammillary bodies of the hypothalamus. These pathways project via the mammillo-thalamic tract to the anterior thalamus, which in turn projects thalamocortical fibers to the cingulate gyrus. See Figure Five.

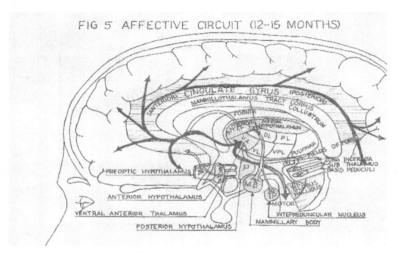

Fig 5. Affective Circuit (12–15 Months)

As part of the development of the gross motor system, fibers are received and integrated at the ventral anterior thalamus from various areas of the neocortex. Involved in this gross motor activity is the development of the fields of Fore to interconnect the globus pallidus with the ventral anterior thalamus, and especially the zona incerta to enhance timing behavior in motor movements.

The interpeduncular nucleus is developing now, as part of the affective circuit that projects fibers from the mammillothalamic tract down to the limbic midbrain area to unite the vegetative functions of the autonomic nervous system with the cingulate. It's considered to be very similar in function to the olfactory 'synchronal' area only on a higher, more complex level.

The posterior cingulate enables vigorous motor activity, so the one-year-old loves the excitement of being chased.[1] The cingulate influences the emotional memory,[2] so that the child learns from past positive or negative experiences what is good and bad and responds appropriately by approaching pleasure and avoiding displeasure.

Stimulation of the cingulate can produce such oral activities as chewing, licking, swallowing, and vocalization; and visceral reactions such as changes in blood pressure, gastric motility, pupillary dilatation, decrease in muscle tone, sleep, and effects similar to vagus nerve stimulation.[3]

The cingulate area is where repression can occur on a higher level of control, as cingulate impulses are sent via the caudate to block thalamic activity causing a suppression of the electrical activity in the neocortex.[4] Thus, a traumatic shock can wipe out a particular memory from conscious recollection, but there remains an emotional fear associated with the distressing event.

This 'affective' circuit is also concerned with the penile erection, and vaginal lubrication.[5] So, the necessity for sociability concerning early sexual activity develops together at this time.

Chapter 22

From 16 through 18 months of age, the 'imagery' response develops and is an aspect of the sensory nervous system. Imagination is essential for creativity and the ability to solve problems; this area makes use of the audio-visual function of imagination.

The 16-month-old child, up until this time, has formed no mental images of his surroundings; as a result, he lived in the present. There is an ability to now create and retain an image that represents the beginning of symbolic thinking.[1]

'*The 16-month-old watches and listens. He is very sensitive to visual and auditory cues which have social meaning. The ability to speak and to understand is accelerating. His imagination creates expectations that cause him to be more demanding now. When he hears someone stirring, he stops what he is doing and changes to a position of alert anticipation. He is becoming very assertive and tends not to get on well with people. He is starting to want to be doing things for himself, asserting his independence.[2]*'

Chapter 23

The 'imagery' circuit refers to the pulvinar and lateral posterior nucleus of the thalamus, and its corresponding association area in the temporal-parietal cortex. The midline nuclei area of the thalamus that provides a new awareness of the senses is developing now, as seen in the diffuse and non-specific sensory feedback of internal and external cues, and non-specific exteroceptors. See Figure Six.

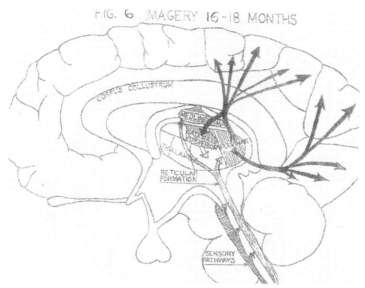

Fig 6. Imagery (16–19 Months)

The area of the pulvinar thalamus has increased its relative size in man, because of its more elaborate integrating sensory function that can provide one of the principle differences between man and animals.[1]

The pulvinar thalamus borders the visual-auditory and somator-sensory cortex and is an ideal position to influence and integrate sensory information.

The audio-visual and somatosensory connection is one of imagining similar things heard, seen, or felt. This imagery leads to possible actions and their possible consequences. This association function of imagination is a diffuse system that permits a creative process to develop.

The ability of the pulvinar, parietal and temporal areas to create audio-visual sensation such as imagery is combined and integrated with the affective memory of the cingulate area to provide the capacity for abstract thinking to develop.

Chapter 24

From nineteen to twenty-one months, the 'action' period develops in the ego and the behaviors of the motor nervous system are growing.

'The one and a half-year-old is a runabout, who is constantly getting into everything. He is impulsive, busy, self-contained, and independent. He likes to chase and be chased, and he enjoys a little roughhousing now. Straining at the leash, he lugs, tugs, pulls, pushes, and pounds. He would rather push his baby carriage now than ride in it.

The 19-month-old endlessly shifts from one thing to another. He likes to go exploring. He discovers by moving about investigating in an exploratory manner. He refuses to be touched, to have his arm held, or be restrained by a playpen, as he needs room to run around.

His attention, like his body activity, is constantly shifting. So, his attention span operates in brief, quick strokes. The 19-month-old finds it difficult to wait because he lives strictly in the present.

Immersed in the here and now, he is blind to anything in the future. He accepts almost any stranger as a companion on excursions. After eating his afternoon meal, he goes right to sleep for a nap. When going to bed at night after an active day, he is easily quieted by being talked to.

He depends on an abundant non-verbal vocabulary of gestures to express himself. He manipulates things with competence and assurance. He completes a situation with a decisive manner that shows an interest in conclusions.

He may treat other children as objects rather than people and poke, pull, push, and pinch them as though they were objects for manipulation. Since people do not give him undue concern, he shows a high degree of self-containment and may play by himself for hours, quite contentedly. He enjoys turning the knob of the radio to play music to dance by, as he may sway his whole body keeping time with a musical rhythm.

If caught taking something he knows he shouldn't, he will run away and drop the object. He may become angry when things don't work out the way he thinks they should, sometimes going into a tantrum with violent crying, hitting, kicking, and casting himself on the floor. When fatigued, he has little desire to control his impulses and is apt to grab objects and go into a tantrum.[1,]

Chapter 25

The 'action' circuit refers to the red nucleus and at the ventral lateral thalamus, where gross motor integration is occurring through which projections from the frontal lobe continue downward to lower motor areas. See Figure 7.

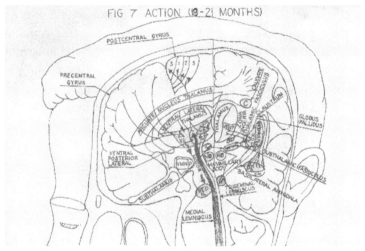

Fig 7. Action (19–21 Months)

The subthalamus nucleus and the zona incerta motor areas are maturing now. These motor areas along with the claustrum play an important function in the rhythm and music ability that is becoming quite evident.

The proprioceptive aspect of the outgoing 'specific' sensory ability is developing. (The incoming 'nonspecific' sensory part solidified during the last 'imagery' period.)

This proprioceptive feedback provides an explicit awareness within the muscle fibers to give control for successful motor action.[1]

The arcuate nucleus and the ventral posterior lateral nucleus of the thalamus integrate outgoing information that receives fibers from the trigeminal and medial lemniscus respectively and projected to the somesthetic gyrus of the parietal cortex.[2,3.]

Chapter 26

From twenty-two months to two years of age, the 'expectancy' response develops in the ego and is an aspect of the sensory nervous system. The 'expectancy' response can be witnessed in an 'orienting reflex' of a house cat when it directs all its senses and concentration toward some sound. With the ability to anticipate, the 'expectancy' response creates a state of readiness, by orienting the senses toward a greater awareness of the surroundings.[1] The 'expectancy' response is the eighth and last growth period and circuit of the ego. At two years of age, the higher self begins its developmental phase.

'The future is starting to have meaning, as the toddler is able to sit at the table and wait for juice. And he is able to respond appropriately to "in a minute."

A concept of space is developing so that he can point or pull a person to show things. He clings to routines and likes to have patterns repeated. He may even have definite demands as to how mother shall speak and act.

This begins a period of sleeping difficulties which may continue to three years of age. Sleep is more disturbed now and there is more night waking.

Difficulties occur not only on going to sleep and during sleep, but also on waking. After going to bed, instead of going to sleep, he may repeatedly call his mother back for numerous demands that whimsically come to mind. There is difficulty in taking a nap also just as it is with night sleeping.

He has a poor command of words, but he has much to say, so in frustration, he "bawls" or throws a tantrum in an unreasonable manner. However, his intense crying is usually because he can't verbalize his wishes which are often for the repetition of certain things.

He responds less quickly to requests and is apt to do the opposite of what is asked of him; for example, he may run in the opposite direction when it is time to go home. He may stand rigid and frozen when told to do something. His inability to verbalize increases his tendency to "freeze" into inactivity.

Earlier toilet training may have a relapse associated with diarrhea. If he has a sudden bowel movement in his pants, he may be unable to move, and stand screaming in distress and continue screaming while being changed.

He likes to undress completely when alone and run about naked. It is a common sight to see a twenty-one without any clothes on.

Since the child, at this age, is sensitive to peripheral stimuli, distractions may interrupt or terminate his meal. And when feeding himself, he eats better alone with his mother moving about close by but not paying attention to him.

He is more conscious of his acts as they are related to the adult's approval and disapproval, as he is both more responsive to and more demanding of adults. He may refuse to return to solitary play after his mother comes to him.

His adjustment to nursery school weakens and waivers, as he may approach other children and hug them too tightly with a bear hug.

He is not only more aware of people than formerly but also knows ·what belongs to different people. He likes to have his own place for his things.

The enjoyment he derives from putting things back in place indicates the categorization and organization going on.[2, ']

Chapter 27

The 'expectancy' circuit, seen in Fig. 8, shows that the dorsomedial thalamus has two-way connections with the basolateral amygdala of the limbic brain and with the orbitofrontal neocortex lobe.

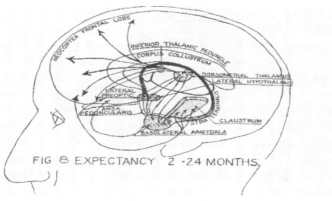

Fig 8. Expectancy (2–24 Months)

The dorsomedial thalamus acts as an intermediate control to combine the emotional impulses of the basolateral amygdala with the frontal area to respond to the external situation in accord with internal needs and to categorize and generalize in a more refined manner.

The frontal lobe augments the emotional and motivational states of the basolateral amygdala with strong anticipatory energy, referred to as 'expectancy waves.[1.]'

The crude relevancy of the basolateral amygdala has now been more refined into the more successful discrimination and generalization ability of the frontal cortex.

In other words, the basolateral amygdala provides the emotional arousal and general direction, while the frontal area increases this energy with greater relevancy, and discrimination; and provides the persistence which memory permits.

The basolateral and the frontal cortex region are a non-verbal communication area that allows one to adapt by learning from mistakes to avoid them in the future.

The attentive process of the 'orienting reflex' operates with greater awareness now as the frontal lobe along with the basolateral amygdala plays a preparative role regarding cognition.[2]

Optimal alerting facilitates perceptual readiness to minimize the surprise for the individual and limits the need for searching by letting the senses do the work of muscles.[3]

For events to be comprehended and labeled, they require a selective attention to the particular aspect of an impulse. This focus is related to expectancy as well as other variables, such as anxiety.[4]

If you know what is to happen, you will be prepared to focus your attention and to perceive and record the events more accurately.

The reticular formation provides the energy and impetus for this sensory modality, as stimulation of the reticular formation enables sensory sensitivity and discrimination.[5,6.]

However, as excitatory impulses increase in the area, avoidance and withdrawal behavior produce introversion, because of the dorsomedial thalamus, which is like the basolateral amygdala, because it is a punishing area where stimulation creates fear and escape reactions.

But the dorsomedial operates the frontal area on a higher level of motor control to express and augment the fear originating from the basolateral amygdala of the limbic brain rather than create the fear itself.[7]

Chapter 28

At the age of two, the development of the ego ends, and the growth of the higher self begins. Some may want to create a nickname for the ego, such as one of the following: Bee; Bo; Bub; Coco; Dee; Harp; Kid; Mo; Pal; Peanut; Pep; Pip; Pup; Sport; Vega; Zeno.

The 'caring' period of the higher self develops from two to two and a half years of age. The ego was not able to develop integrity because the physical configuration of the circuits of its eight growth periods is discrete and separate. At this time, the past eight circuits of the ego travel en masse up via a neural pathway to the thalamus of the higher self, where they are integrated to operate together as one behavior, and their unity produces integrity in the child.[1]

At two, this integrity creates the ability to love that emanates from within the child that before had to be elicited from the love of a caregiver. The other periods of development for the higher self happen again at the ages of twelve to fifteen, from twenty-two to twenty-five, and from thirty-two to thirty-five years of age.

During this early period of the higher self's development, the child needs a negative stubbornness to protect himself against overstimulating situations.[2] He may protest against everything more as a sign of his vulnerability, rather than being rebellious or making trouble. This hard-outer shell he creates protects the softness inside.

'This period is when words are undergoing rapid expansion. The child talks to himself, repeats words, and names things with a compelling urge, in order to exercise his new vocal ability. With a new interest in verbal interactions, he now enjoys listening to his mother's conversation and contributes a few comments of his own.

His developing ability to walk and talk creates a problem because others tend to overestimate his capacity and expect too much of him.

Although he mostly enjoys playing alone, he likes to affectionately approach other children to hug, kiss, and tenderly pal them. And this is the time when affection for the parents is shown. A real display of affection towards his mother is especially strong at bedtime.

This affection may spread to other adults. Even his voice has affective tones. And he may take affectionate care of his toys. In nursery play, children of this age laugh together with eddies and bursts of contagious humor.

His sensitivity is beginning to interfere with his sleep. Leaving the door open slightly when going to bed with a night light can relieve some of the child's anxiety of the door acting as a barrier separating the child from his mother. He may get out of bed many times because of loneliness. Or he may feel the sensations to urinate many times, even though he won't be able to urinate.

The two-year-old child prefers a relationship with one adult, as two people create too many difficulties. When with a group of people, he may possessively demand all his mother's time and attention.

His strong demands around the home are in marked contrast to the compliance and meekness away from home.

His increasing sensitivity to people causes him to be shy with strangers, and he may hide behind his mother's skirt.

The two-year-old is more cautious and conservative than before. He is comfortable with the familiar; whereas the new or strange may baffle or disturb him.

He understands the property rights of others so he is not getting into so many things, but he wants to own as many things as he can. He may be under the impression that just a claim of ownership establishes something as his own since that's what the adults appear to do.

He does not like to share and tends to hoard what is his. Instead of letting someone else play with his things, he prefers to find substitutes for others to use.

The fights over play material seldom allow cooperative play to develop. He prefers to intently watch what others are doing rather than participate. And he still prefers solitary play in this pre-cooperative stage. He is happiest in his play with books, music, and a soft animal toy

The child at this stage has a genuine interest in the mother-baby relationship and becomes engrossed in doll play or imitating feminine household activities. The father is the favorite now, although he will want his mother if he is in trouble or tired.

The child has to organize his experience through touching, handling, hoarding, fleeing, and pursuing. He goes briefly from one activity to another as he did at eighteen months, but these short spells of activities are more organized. And the process of the organization goes on with the variations on each repetition.[3.]

Chapter 29

The 'care' circuit of the higher self from two to two-and-a-half-year-old child can be seen in Figure 9. This is an integrating region where the septal area of the thalamus is the primary integrating unit that unites or ties together the ego's past eight growth periods of development.

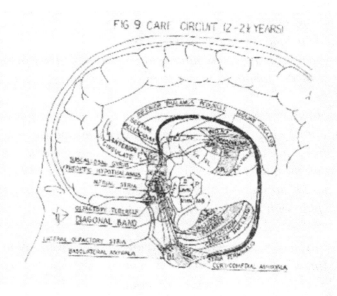

Fig 9. Care Circuit (2–2½ Years)

The 'care' circuit refers to the diagonal band, the medial olfactory stria, the intralamina nuclei of the thalamus, the septal area (para-olfactory or Brocal area), and the subcallosal gyrus.

To facilitate the integration of these eight separate circuits, the septal has the pathways, structural ability, and location to coordinate these many tracts simultaneously.

For example, the caudate nucleus, the putamen, and the claustrum send fibers to the frontal area to influence the integration of inhibitory motor response in the septal. The diagonal band connects the putamen, the globus pallidus, and the corticomedial amygdala to the septal.

The basolateral amygdala sends fibers by way of the ventral amygdalofugal tract to join the diagonal band and the septal.

The dorsomedial thalamus sends fibers to the septal via the inferior thalamic peduncle to integrate discrimination and generalization functions and avoidance responses.

All of these areas combine to create a powerful inhibitory effect on autonomic and somatomotor responses. This integration allows a greater capacity to suppress learned responses that are inappropriate and thus enhance problem-solving ability.

The para-olfactory and septal area is an important speech area, and it is at this time that speech begins to blossom, the child discards jargon and begins to speak in sentences.

Association fibers and association nuclei of the thalamus, integrate thalamic activity, the inferior thalamic peduncle, and the intralamina nuclei of the thalamus, all receives sensory input and project fibers to the orbital frontal cortex and the septal to coordinate thalamic activity with the septal region.

Further integration occurs within the septal area as the anterior cingulate gyrus becomes continuous with the subcallosal and septal areas. The medial stria from the olfactory area integrates this area with the septal; the stria terminalis hooks up the septal with the corticomedial amygdala, and finally, the preoptic area of the hypothalamus becomes continuous with the septal to provide intimate connections with the hypothalamus.

These areas are united at the septal to integrate emotional effect with anticipation and imagination. Imaginativeness, expectancy, and excitement are used as energy sources to create more intense highs and lows in pleasure and displeasure.[1]

The 'care' area, concentrated in the septal, acts as an energy booster by coordinating these past various circuits together and utilizing their different energies in a more adaptive and more efficient manner.

Although the septal has punishing sites, it primarily combines other displeasure areas and integrates them with other behaviors, e.g. anticipation. As a result, this is the period when anxiety is reaching its peak of intensity.

Reward centers can also be found within the 'care' circuitry, especially in the septal, to make this an intensely pleasurable area.

Chapter 30

The development of the higher self continues now from two-and-a-half to three years of age and is a willful or goal-directed age. Spankings and punishment are reaching a peak at this time because it is the most exasperating age of all to adults. This period of development is often referred to as the 'terrible twos,' because he tries his parents with contrary extremes.

'Yes and No! Come and go, run and stop, give and take, push and pull, assault and retreat, are some of his behaviors that can represent the range of his desires.

He may demand to be fed, then turn around and refuse to eat. He may change from being very active to being passively peaceful or be screaming loudly one moment and mutter in a soft whisper the next.

His enthusiastic helpfulness and sociability may suddenly shift to a desire to withdraw into isolation.

He is caught between alternatives that at 18 months were not so desirable or pressing, and the avoidance and shyness of 24 months now include their opposite behaviors of approach and aggressiveness. He needs to try both ways to find out which is best for him.

Children at this age want to be with other people, but their intrinsic excitability makes it difficult for them to handle people. They usually play best with one other child, especially one who is older that he can respect and accept.

When children of this age come together in nursery school, it creates a conglomeration of the extremes of sociality. The play is mainly self-centered with each independently following his own devices, but the rudiments of cooperation are beginning to form in parallel activity. And the desire of each to imitate the other is developing a kind of mutual collaboration that is creating a social bond. He may eagerly show playmates his favorite toys but can't bring himself to let go of them and share them with the others.

He doesn't have the overflowing warmth of the two-year-old, as his affections have taken on more of a detached superficiality. Affection often is expressed in a rigid form, such as a kissing ritual. Something keenly desired may be ignored with indifference once it is possessed, and his mother may be dismissed from the nursery with a thoughtless "goodbye."

His growing independence is shown in his behavior on walks as he either runs ahead or lags behind. When he knows what he wants, he can make strong demands, and go after it with determined dispatch. He may ask his mother to leave the room when he feeds himself for part of a meal, or when he goes to the bathroom. He may throw a temper tantrum over dressing conflicts, and he may not permit his mother to touch him when he insists on dressing himself.

At two-and-a-half years old, an interest in an imaginary playmate comes spontaneously from within the child. This internal relationship will usually reflect and satisfy some inner need, whether it is for companionship, someone to beat, someone to look up to, someone to do things for or someone to boss. Sometimes his identity may shift at two-and-a-half to become an animal.

When alone, his activity is accompanied by constant talking. Speech, the motor expression of his experiences, is now put into practice within the security of his private room, or at bedtime when he may talk to his teddy bear.

When being put to bed, he likes to have things in their proper place. His tenaciousness is making him resistant to change and he may fly into a temper tantrum when his routine is disrupted.

All is not well with the world of the two-and-a-half-year-old. He does not laugh quite freely. He takes himself too seriously because he is caught in the rigidities of ritualism, perseverance, and negativism. His domineering manner may be hard for others to accept. He verbally asserts his domination over other members of the family. He may command one to sit here, another to do something else, and still another to go away.

His imperial demands show a new excitable energy source that provides a determination that can be helpful in putting things away, carrying out simple tasks around the house, and going on errands. This energy comes from within himself so he cannot be forced; he can only be activated in the right direction.

His new vigor and easy arousal are causing difficulties in relaxing readily to go to sleep. When scheduled to take a nap, he usually consumes over an hour in different self-activities. He may get in and out of the bed several times, before finally going to sleep.

The two-and-a-half-year-old may express jealousy toward younger siblings. His intense energy causes stuttering, high tension, and sudden fatigue. He is proud of his ability to do things. And his energy allows him to do things he could never do before.[1.]

Chapter 31

The 'goal-directed' circuit called the medial forebrain bundle (MFB) of the higher self is developing now in the two-and-a-half three-year-old child. See Figure 10.

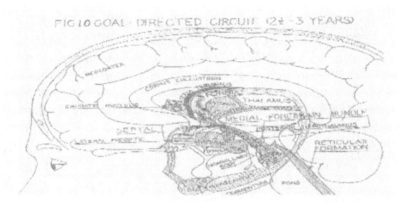

Fig 10. Goal-Directed Circuit (2½–3 Years)

The highly motivating reward area of the MFB deals with goal-directed behavior. This 'goal-directed' circuit is concerned with goals that are an expression of the oral and genital functions essential for self-preservation and the preservation of the species.[1]

The neural pattern of this circuit develops again in the fourth layer of the neocortex around twelve-and-a-half years of age and initiates the sexual development at the early stage of puberty. The variations of the beginning of puberty would indicate if a person's rate of growth is normal, or if one is an early or late bloomer.

In your hemisphere (the logical, rational self), your reproductive circuits would be reaching a sexual peak between seventeen-and-a-half and eighteen years of age. There are also sexual peaks at twenty-three, twenty-eight, thirty-three, and thirty-eight years of age that occur with decreasing levels of vitality.

Fibers from the reticular formation, mediated by the lateral region of the hypothalamus, are carried in the MFB to provide tremendous energy and provide an action system that can make the individual restless and full of desire to be doing something.

The descending reticular formation arouses motor pathways in the lower brain stem to influence motor activity and a constant low-level activity of the body tissue, especially in muscle tone.

As long as the individual is actively pursuing a goal, then the control exerted by the innervation of the reticular formation in the midbrain region can reduce excitation to a tolerable level so that the individual is able to handle anxiety more effectively.[2,3,4.]

While the energizing ascending reticular formation provides arousal and alertness; it also acts as a motivational apparatus to provide the driving impetus needed for muscular activity.

The extensive and diffused interaction of the MFB provides a greater period of integration than the prior period, as the autonomic and motor components of the lower brainstem, mediated by the hypothalamus, are brought into a union of activity with the 'care' region by the MFB to channel arousal into specific directions.[5]

Chapter 32

The 'stabilizing' period of growth by the three to four years old higher self is now developing. The higher self is now showing a new ability to engage in cooperative play with other children. The three-year-old has himself well in hand with emotional and physical self-control.

'He is no longer as paradoxical and unpredictable as he was at two-and-a-half years. Instead of the contrariness of the past, this is a time when he tries to please and conform, and he is most pleased when he pleases others.

The three-year-old's "higher self" is at an imitative and social age and is making important distinctions between physical obstacles and personal ones. He is becoming mildly affectionate, and the expression of emotions, such as sympathy, is becoming more apparent. With a strong tendency to establish social contacts, he likes to visit a friend's house during the day.

The three-year-old's free play is less reckless and rash, than it was in the last period. Self-dependence and sociability are more balanced to help him to fit in more comfortably with others around him.

Although he is capable of self-initiative, he tends to be influenced more by social suggestion. He is more susceptible to praise, so suggestions are more useful than direct orders. In fact, he may do things he does not like to do if he is given a good reason. He gladly helps his mother put his toys away and will go to the toilet on a slight suggestion.

The conflicting extremes of half a year ago give way to a high degree of self-control. His greater restraint has its basis in motor responses, and his motor expressions are more evenly balanced and fluid.

The smooth and cooperative play of a group of three-year-olds is more spontaneous yet more calm and self-reliant compared to the stormy two and a half-year-old group. Several children are likely to participate together in some type of activity with much laughter and verbal humor accompanying play.

Since the gross motor drive is under the child's control, there is a greater freedom with fewer environmental restrictions.

He enjoys helping others when he can. His growing self-reliance allows him to help in small household tasks and to help in getting his room in order.

The three-year-old is proud of his own increasing abilities and is more capable of solving his own problems now.

The adjustment problems of the three-year-old are infrequent. His time-consuming demands are lessening as a more cooperative adaptiveness is developing. There is not the need of rituals for self-protection because his personal relations are more flexible.

His advances in his ability to handle personal-social relationships are one of the most difficult and complicated tasks that the growing child will have to encounter.

Because the three-year-old is less turned in on himself emotionally, he is surer of himself and superficially shows some savoir-faire.

His motor action system is in a state of equilibrium so that everything is working together effectively. He is becoming a man of the world displaying a certain flair when he makes his entrance into the nursery.

And he may occasionally shout and sing with exuberant confidence. Three-year-olds may insult each other and use swear words to indicate that they are not afraid to be a little bad.

He has developed the ability to judge and is ready to choose between two competing alternatives. Instead of the doubt of before, he can now enjoy making a choice within the realm of his experience.

When walking into the nursery, he may survey the situation for a moment and then with deliberateness choose a child or an activity that he is interested in.

The three-year-old is developing an ability to limit his interest to a smaller area, and he is able to focus his attention and interest longer.

The daily routines do not have to be rushed as before. He can make easy transitions and adaptations because he can wait his turn. One can bargain with him now because he can delay doing the things he wants to do and hold himself in anticipation.

If he cannot fall asleep during naptime, then he is content to play at "napping." If he inquires and finds out that the required time to sleep is not up, then he will usually return to his "play napping" without protest.

Memories of his past babyhood are relieved at this age as he likes to recall his past experiences and achievements. His memory process is actively felt as he is bursting with interesting stories about his home experiences even before he enters the nursery. With a new confidence in his utterance, he has an eager desire to talk, and if encouraged, some could talk indefinitely.

If he has confidence in the security of the routine, then he can shed his dependence on his mother with an indifferent goodbye on entering the nursery.

When the parents leave him to go "out" when at home, he may cry until he vomits, or until the parents return.

The mother is the more favored parent now. The three-year-old clings less at bedtime and usually falls asleep more quickly than at two two-and-a-half years. He is beginning to report dreams.

His imaginative life reaches a peak at three and a half years in the form of an imaginary playmate. He relates this imaginary companion intimately with his activities and home life, so that the imaginary playmate may have a place at the table, go for a ride in the car, and sleep in or under the child's bed.

The child is often very demanding about the rights of his imaginary companion and very solicitous in teaching him many things. Although he does not bring the companion into the nursery school, he may bring him as far as the nursery door.[1,]

Chapter 33

The 'stabilizing' circuit of the three to four-year-old child represents the next developmental period of the higher self, as seen in Figure 11.

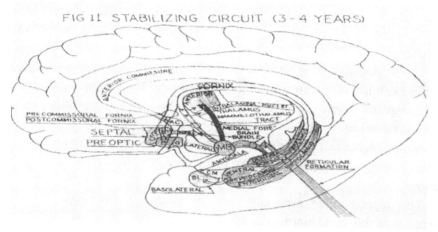

Fig 11. Stabilizing Circuit (3–4 Years)

There are two primary divisions within this 'stabilizing' circuit, each with different functions. The dorsal hippocampus sends fibers to and from the mammillary body by way of the post commissural division of the fornix; while the other division is the pre-commissural fornix which contains fibers from the ventral hippocampus that project them to the septal.[1]

The ventral hippocampal fibers that connect the septal area and inhibit the sensory (arousal) nervous system while the fibers from the dorsal hippocampus that connect the mammillary body restrain the motor/muscle (arousal) nervous system.

The hippocampus participates directly in making the memory stronger in a consolidation process. The hippocampus, working in conjunction with the entorhinal area, operates as an intermediator to retrieve memories impressed on the cells by the absorptive ability of the sensory nervous system. On the other hand, the retrieval of memory from storage depends on the 'projection' ability of the motor aspect of the hippocampus.[2,3.]

In other words, to effectively lay down a memory into a storage area depends on the emotional implications and 'meaning' that can make a strong impression on sensory cells of the sensory (arousal) system. The retrieval of memory in storage depends on the motor (arousal) system so that the sensory impressions are 'projected' from the entorhinal-hippocampal areas outward.

Imagination aids memory by creating a reverberating feedback where impressions and 'projections' oscillate rapidly back and forth, as the input and output aspects are completed in a circuit and then gradually consolidated by this echo process.

The hippocampus has long-lasting inhibitory effects that reduce cell excitability. And one of the most important behaviors that the hippocampus develops during the 'stabilizing' period is the ability to inhibit arousal in this early stage.

The hippocampus has diffused two-way connections with the amygdala of the limbic brain, so it can control the excitation of the basolateral division of the amygdala which has significant connections with the pituitary-adrenal stress mechanism.[4]

So, the higher self is now evolving into an ability to hinder or prevent some of the thoughts coming from the ego that would otherwise result in misguided actions.

The hippocampus especially has an inhibitory influence on ACTH secretion of this rapid alarm system.[5,6,7.]

The reticular formation innervates the hippocampus in the early stages of attention, and in turn, the hippocampus restrains arousal from the reticular formation, so they become a mutually inhibitory relationship.[4.]

Basket cells in the hippocampus have feedback pathways that reduce excitation, so that the more the pyramidal cells fire, the more it activates the feedback inhibition that stops cellular firing. Whether an axon conducts impulses is decided by the basket cell neurons.[8]

Basket cells not only keeps down the level of excitation, but effectively participate in cell integration that can modify patterns of neuronal responses by shaping impulses into specific forms of neural performance.[9]

So, the hippocampus seems to have the function of analyzing sensory input for relevant information regarding experience and the current situation. It can inhibit unwanted responses and exploratory behavior and allow appropriate responses and appropriate exploratory behavior, and proper responses to novel stimuli.

The hippocampus expanded, grew and evolved over the ages, and over many millenniums, to create the neocortex. Now the hippocampus acts as the neocortex of the ego's limbic subcortical brain.

In contrast to the inflexibility of the basolateral amygdala rhythms, the hippocampal rhythms have an exquisite plasticity.

The frequencies of the hippocampal rhythms vary from three to seven cycles per second (cps) theta waves to the fast beta waves of 40 cps by providing different degrees of synchronization and random firing in its cells. The hippocampus represents the highest level of control for the innervation and suppression of excitatory impulses below the neocortical level.

The frequency of the hippocampus rhythm seems to be a function of the degree of motivation.[10] The motivational behavior of arousal occurs when the slow theta rhythm of the hippocampus inactivates the hippocampus to permit maximum attention and EEG arousal of the neocortex. Fast beta waves of 30–40 cps in the hippocampus inhibit the reticular formation to reduce arousal in the neocortex.

The 'stabilizing' response of the hippocampus tends to maintain a kind of emotional equilibrium. When the neocortex shows a negligible EEG arousal with alpha waves, the hippocampus can elevate one's mood to prevent drowsiness and maintain a state of stability. In the opposite sense, the hippocampus calms an overly aroused person down to maintain a balanced equilibrium.

The hippocampus is capable of keeping one near the center on a horizontal plane to maintain a stability between the parasympathetic and the sympathetic nervous systems and on a vertical plane between pleasure and displeasure in the sensory (arousal) system. Thus, the hippocampus allows one to maintain a 'stabilizing' state of equilibrium.

The hippocampus is also able to inhibit excessive energy that causes displeasure from the basolateral amygdala. The hippocampus can either inhibit the energy impulses or redirect the energy. So, this energy can be used in the motor (arousal) nervous system for action, or in the sensory (arousal) system for pleasure or learning, according to one's motivational choice.

Severing an animal's fornix produced an excessively emotional reaction.[11] A monkey reacted with chronic ferocity from bilateral hippocampus lesions.[12]

Excitatory hyperactivity was so compelling in rats with dorsal hippocampal lesions that they could not stay on a 'safe' platform to keep from being shocked.[13]

Hydrophobia or rabies destroys the inhibitory cells of the hippocampus, neocortex, and motor pathways. It results in extreme fear where a slight sensory stimulus can bring on convulsions of fear, demonstrated by spasms of the larynx and pharynx. Intense seizures paralyze breathing and death results.

Bilateral lesions of the hippocampus cause a memory loss of verbal and non-verbal material even if the patients let their attention wander for one-second.

In Korsakoff's psychosis, there is a degeneration of the hippocampus, fornix and mammillary bodies resulting in gross memory defects and an inability to learn or retain new facts and skills.[14.]

In this psychotic reaction, there are acute fear, hallucinations, disorientation, suggestibility and tremor. This is seen in chronic alcoholism that can cause a psychotic reaction, such as an attack of DTs or delirium tremens.

Patients who suffer from this, acquired less information and forgot it faster; they quickly lost new associations, and there was no relearning. They could not handle any learning task that involved more than two items. There seemed to be two underlying disabilities, a fragmentary impression of events that had no association with the experience, and a fixation on a limited set of behavioral responses.

Chapter 34

This 'sociable' growth period of the higher self from four to five years of age is very versatile. The four-year-old is a genuinely social being, and not only wants to join a playgroup every morning but intends to be with playmates every afternoon.

'What can he not do? He can be quiet, noisy, calm, assertive, cozy, imperious, suggestible, social, independent, athletic, artistic, literal, fanciful, cooperative, indifferent, inquisitive, forthright, prolix, humorous, dogmatic, silly, competitive.

His blithe and lively activity pattern and contrariness are typical of the two to three-year-old. But this is not a regression; the mental behavioral achievements at the age of three serves to stabilize, and he is now functioning at a higher, more adaptive level in all the motor, language, and personal anti-social areas of his behavior.

If at times, he seems somewhat voluble, dogmatic, boastful and bossy, it is because he is a blithe amateur swinging into fresh fields of self-expression.

He prefers a very creative dramatic type of play where his ability to shift rapidly allows him to play his "roles" with a facile ease. Through social dramatic play, he is striving to identify himself with his culture and to assimilate it into his world of behaviors.

He likes to dress up and act like an adult, often with excellent behavioral imitation and acting ability. This play-acting is a most effective way of maturing and shows he is more interested in being socialized into the culture, rather than having a resistance to it.

He is most happy when with one adult. And his endless questioning is not so much a pursuit of knowledge as a social device to practice speech and listening behaviors. He likes to make faces to identify with adults and improve his skills using facial expressions. These expressions are used as a way to understand and incorporate the complexities of his culture.

While the three-year-old had a conforming mind, the four-year-old has a fluent, lively mind. His high drive combined with a fluid mental organization provides the key to understand the four-year-old. His mental effervescence and fluid flights of fancy make it possible for him to dramatize any experience, besides making him a good fabricator of alibis.

His mental agility provides a diffuse ability to use words with an abandoned ease. He is excessive in his speech. He may exhaust every verbal possibility while running a topic into the ground

He is a great talker who is believable, because his burgeoning language often camouflages his lack of knowledge. A kind of dramatic poet, he enjoys learning new and different words, especially for their humorous affect. Verbal and physical exaggerations amuse him as he is showing off on the trapezes with flying commentary.

Another key to understanding the four-year-old is his high-energy drive associated with his extremely mobile mental organization. While the three-year-old was agreeable and compliant, the four-year-old is assertive and expansive.

He surges ahead with both muscles and mind. He tells tall tales; he brags; he tattles; he threatens; he alibis; he calls names.

He is proud of his creations and achievements and praises himself by a boastfulness that reaches its highest level.

He resists confinement around the home and is trying out his newfound powers. It is the four-year-old who runs away from home.

Relatively self-sufficient, he enjoys his times alone, which can be a very creative period. With more self-control, he can do two things at one time and no longer has to stop midway in what he is doing when he begins to talk.

He may be jealous of his mother and father together. He expresses strong affection at bedtime and falls asleep rather quickly.

He can take a preparatory nap to stay up late in the evening in contrast to the two to three-year-old who will become so excited that he will be unable to sleep. He wakes up in a happy mood, greets his parents with conversation instead of the romping abandon of a year ago.

And his imaginary companion takes part in his dramatic social play that is closer to the realms of likelihood.[1,]

Chapter 35

This growth period of the higher self from four to five years of age shows how the habenula brings together and integrates the past eleven stages of circuit development. The habenula nucleus and its many tracts constitute the 'integrative' circuit, as seen in Figure 12.

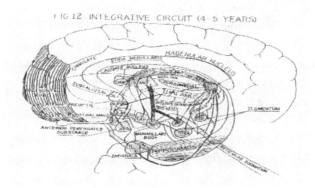

Fig 12. Integrative Circuit (4–5 Years)

One of the habenula tracts, referred to as the stria medullaris, connects the same nuclei as the medial forebrain bundle (MFB) of the 'goal-directed' circuit, including the interconnections between many of the hypothalamic nuclei, although the MFB by-passes the habenula.[1]

The stria medullaris is the primary input system of the habenula complex. Since the MFB connects the same nuclei as the stria medullaris, then it would follow that this 'goal-directed' activity is the key behavior to innervate the habenula.

Some of the other habenula tracts hook up the 'synchronal' area, the midline, and dorsomedial thalamus to the prefrontal lobe, the hippocampal area, the amygdala complex, the mammillary bodies, the anterior thalamus, the interpeduncular nucleus with the cingulate, and the limbic midbrain areas.[2,3]

Chapter 36

The neocortex, the gray matter of the brain, is divided into six layers. The first three layers are solidified or 'locked in' at ten-years of age. The fourth layer of the brain represents the sensory nervous system (N.S.) and develops from ten to twenty years of age; the effects of the sensory N.S. can be seen in teens' disposition to be a night owl with a desire to stay up late, and objecting to getting out of bed in the morning. They tend to be very curious, and their sensitivity often causes them to retreat to their bedroom as they prefer to be alone.

During the twenties, the fifth layer of the neocortex represents the motor N.S. This is the period when muscle development reaches its peak and when athletes are achieving their prime in their physical abilities and performances.

During the thirties, the sixth or top layer of the neocortex develops with the autonomic N.S. being predominate. This is the age when people start to develop a gut and 'love handles,' and have a stronger desire to settle down, get married, and raise a family.[1,2,3.]

Part Three

Chapter 37

Children have a joy for life and bring feelings of love and goodwill. They promote what is just and right in all areas of life. Their joyfulness for life is not lost in the unhappiness of the world even in the face of misery, their cheerfulness for living persist. In these young ones, an honest world still exists, as they willingly strive for what is good. These hopeful children are owed all our attention and love from us all.

****

Nothing is more important to the child than learning, the experiences arising from it, and the practical knowledge gained from living. These moments of learning are the most decisive phases of the life of a youngster. Thus, it's essential that children provide their own particular, individual, comprehensive education, where they can acquire knowledge, and where they can personally realize love, inner freedom, inner harmony, and other positive values on their own.

Some think that being a good parent means being strict, pedantic, or didactic. These adults can have a significant effect that can deprive these children of discovering their real selves. When youngsters depend on others to tell them how to be; then there is no creative effort to shape their unique path, and what they make of themselves is no longer an option that is available to them.

The children must find and learn the truth about themselves, for themselves. This early beginning makes up the crucial years, during which they take in, work out and evaluate the most important things for their life. The personal insights and instincts acquired during this resolute time shapes their life and has a profound influence upon the course of the rest of their existence. Unfortunately, the majority of the grown-ups are not accomplished and skillful at teaching the higher values of life to the young, because they have never grasped them for themselves.

****

The way I understand the 'soul' is, it guides by acting as our muse and directs us to move into certain fields with inspirational guidance. After many lifetimes, the 'soul' will develop abilities or talents in certain areas, like poetry, writing, music, art, invention, mechanical innovation, etcetera, and will be a creative influence in the choices a child makes in life. The 'soul' has no voice but conveys its intentions with enthused feelings about specific area or abilities through the higher self.

Through their own, inner-guidance, children must establish their unique nature and be in charge of their personal growth, because the parents, grandparents, teachers, and others, such as religions, philosophies, military, and governments are not capable of fulfilling this responsibility to instruct them.

Many of these adults will be a prisoner of their ego, a captive of their own point of view, their own thoughts and feelings; and they will be intoxicated by their own speech, and not realize that their ego is guiding them into delusion and confusing which will mislead a child.

Some adults will create an inability to understanding the difference between lies and truth, love and fornication, peace and war, wisdom and imagination, and illusion and reality. Many adults are afraid of the truth and are more concerned that the truth will cause damage to their self-image and their vain worldly endeavors.

To children, it doesn't matter whether one is rich or poor, black or white, because they only want a friendly companion to associate with them. Because of the interference of adults, the older they become, the less value they place on the real values of life, such as love, peace, freedom, harmony, goodness, and character.

So, their relationships get off-course and are frequently dissolved in strife and discord. Friendships and marriages can tun into a profitable connection. A real endurable connection becomes a rarity, because differences about race and religion and financial matters created by the adult's ego emerge, which are hard to overcome because of the ego's desire to react with hate, revenge, and jealousy. These are the absurdities that adults impose on the young so that with maturity the more important values are forgotten.

A child should know the outer world they live in and have an understanding of the inner world of the self. Namely, they should know about the rational self, the higher self, the ego, and the body. When informed about the ego, a child can evolve, mature, and flourish.

Knowledge about the ego applies to a child's relationships and family. With an understanding of the ego, a family can develop, grow and thrive. This knowledge can reduce the tensions and conflicts within a family, between a couple, and within the self to create a foundation upon which emotional maturity and reality can grow.

****

A dysfunctional family or a dysfunctional relationship occurs when there is no understanding about the ego and how its disruptive desires and criticisms create conflicts. The ego thrives on turmoil, arguments, and fights among siblings and couples, as this strengthen its access to their minds and fortify its control. The drama the ego conveys, inhibits rational thinking and decent behavior. With an understanding of how the ego dominates through tricks and manipulation, it allows us to block its maneuvers so we can establish our authority and enjoy supportive relationships.

Children can use the knowledge and behavioral tools presented here to control the ego the rest of their lives, which will set them on a path where they can flourish. Once the ego's beliefs are recognized and corrected with awareness, and they realize their ability to command the ego, then a happy and satisfying life can be experienced with a family and with relationships. This knowledge can reduce the stress and conflict level in their relations to enable them to get along and enjoy life socially.

Chapter 38

The world is socially flawed. This can be altered if people know the behavioral skills that can block the ego's control of their minds with awareness, know that they can direct their ego to obey their intentions, and that they are responsible for the way the ego thinks and the well-being of the other selves.

A primary purpose of this book is to show people how to live. I don't think life should be mysterious and confusing. We lead such short lives that it can take too much time to develop the knowledge and the behavior skills to experience an enjoyable life; and when they do acquire this understanding, then many are too old to reap the benefits of these experiences. Whereas, if they have this information when they are younger, they have many more opportunities to grow and blossom into areas that can add more joy and meaning to their life.

****

People with a privileged life and many in authority seem to have everything but lead lives that are mystifyingly uneasy with many problems and troubles. Those driven to accumulate wealth often find that money doesn't provide the fulfilling life they were expecting. They can often lead a troubled life. Those who acquire wealth and fame at an early age or early adulthood, do not know how to handle their newfound fortune and prominence and turn to addictions, suicide, or something outside of themselves because they've never learned about their own unique abilities to handle personal difficulty. As a result, too many may experience an early death, because of their lack of knowledge about the ego and lack of understanding of how much personal power and authority they possess. With no understanding of the ego, it will be hard for them to develop the skills of awareness that could restrict, contain, and control the ego to enable them to enjoy a fortunate life.

****

When an oxygen molecule loses an electron, it becomes a free radical, called an ion. Free radicals play a significant role in some biological processes. Many of these are necessary for life. When you have an excess of free radical, they can create infections, inflammations, and pain. Free radicals are produced by feeling too cold and shivering, tiring yourself out physically with too much exercise, lack of sleep, overeating to cause undigested food particles to circulate in the bloodstream; with electromagnetic fields (EMF) from cell phone and being in homes and buildings with Wi-Fi; or by allowing the ego to create too much chronic emotional distress and pain. Any of these activities can generate an excess of free radicals.

When a significant number of electrons have been stripped away from your body because of these types of stresses, then the body develops a positive charge and creates an unhealthy state that can make you feel awful with lethargy, brain fog, inflammation, and pain which can affect your enjoyment in life and your relationships with others.

Too many free radicals can cause cell damage, such as inflammation, infections, damage to body tissues and pain. With excessive amounts of free radicals, they can lead to diseases and death, like cancer, stroke, myocardial infarction, diabetes and other major disorders.

If you have trouble with inflammation, infections, and pain, you most likely have too many free radicals. Your body has lost too many electrons to give your body a positive charge which can have a detrimental effect on your emotional connections and relationships with others and needs to be corrected.

Red blood cells have a negative charge that causes them to separate, as like charges cause red blood cells to repel each other. But when the body has too many free radicals, it will become positively charged and will cause many red blood cells to become positively charged. This will cause them to start sticking or clumping together and cause clots to form in the bloodstream. This reduces the ability of the red blood cells to supply your body with oxygen effectively and could even lead to a stroke.

There is a remedial action you can take when your body has lost too many electrons and it's positively charged. There is a great abundance of free electrons in the earth to give the ground a negatively charged potential opposite your body's positively charged state. This imbalance of electric charges causes free electrons to flow from the ground into your body to create a balance that reduces an overabundance of free radicals.

Contact with the earth's surface can recharge your body with free electrons. But this can't happen if you're wearing rubber soles on your shoes or walk on blacktop which is a form of insulation that isolates you from the earth's negative charge. You can wear leather soles, moccasins, sit, lay down, or walk barefooted on any ground surface to recharge your body with free electrons. When in a lightning storm, standing on a blacktop surface can provide protection for you.

We all need to get out and enjoy ourselves in the great outdoors without sunscreen for 30 minutes a day. Contact with the earth will cause free electrons to flow into your body to bring you back to a balanced state that can reduce or even eliminate inflammation and pain. Contact with the land is referred to as 'earthing' or 'grounding. [1,2,3,4,5,6.]

****

Flowers and plants can also exchange free electrons with the electromagnetic field or aura of your body. At a fitness gym, there were six, three-foot tall plants in a bed of soil that surrounded columns. Three of the plants were on the opposite side of the three plants next to where people sat.

The plants next to the people were wilted and dying, while the three plants five feet away were robust and thriving. The manager was informed; we switched the plants, and within a week, they were all flourishing. Plants help us out by removing the harmful stresses within the aura that surround our bodies and helps us feel better.

Women love to receive flowers or a plant because it lifts their spirit. Women are more aware and sensitive to these feelings than men. So, it is harder for men to be aware of this benefit. This awareness is because the corpus callosum pathways are more energized, active, and larger in women than men.

****

The corpus callosum is a major bundle of nerve fibers in the brain that connects you with the ego and the higher self. The corpus callosum is the only way you have to communicate with the ego and the higher self. And the corpus callosum is the only way the ego and the higher self have to communicate with you.[7,8.]

Because the corpus callosum is more active and larger in women than men, the ego has much greater access to women's minds; this will cause women to have more trouble controlling the ego, compared to men.[9,10.]

Perhaps, intuitively, the effects of estrogen create a key that can open up the corpus callosum to provide an easier neural pathway for women to make the higher self and the ego more accessible to women. This greater access to the ego by women will cause them to have more trouble controlling the ego, compared to men.

The smaller corpus callosum in men or the motor nervous system's influence of testosterone lessens the access men have to the ego and the higher self. So, they deal with less emotional stress than women, comparatively speaking.

The ego's greater access to women's minds compels them to recognize the effectiveness of mindfulness more than men because of the many irrational thoughts that come into their heads. Many women discover the importance of awareness on their own, as it makes their lives more manageable. They appreciate the beauty in nature, a sunset, enjoy the beautiful surroundings around their home, etcetera, this awareness makes their life calmer.

Women's corpus callosum allows them greater access to the higher self, which explains their more loving nature, their considerable creativity, their more affectionate, nurturing characteristics, and their increased sensitivity. This increased access to the higher self allows women to 'think outside the box' to creatively solve problems. This greater doorway into the higher self for women permits them to enjoy acts of creativity, like dancing, art, playful fun, and joking around with humor. And this is why women are more gregarious and enjoy dancing more than men.

A woman who develops the skills to control the ego will be emotionally, socially, and mentally stronger than a man. Her easier access to the higher self means she has more significant resources available to her to creatively solve problems and has more access to generalized thinking. A woman who rules herself is capable of having more inherent possibilities than a man. If she's not able to control her ego, she can potentially be worse off than a man.

Chapter 39

When you are skeptical of information you hear and think it is false, the ego will regard the information as true. The ego believes what it views and hears. A statement perceived by the ego is a statement believed. When the ego listens to a falsehood or a lie and remembers it later, it will regard the story or fabrication as truthful. When the ego hears a lie repeatedly, it becomes an absolute fact to the ego.

Since the ego controls our minds and resides in our heads most of the day, the ego erodes and wears away our beliefs, and misleads us about the world around us. The more the ego has command of the mind, the more its ideas influences and controls us. If we are not aware of our egos' lack of realism, we are more likely to be misled and believe a lie is real; this is because of its manipulative adeptness, and the amount of time the ego occupies our mind. This lack of knowledge about the ego allows it to rule by default.

The intent of a half-truth is to misrepresent a truth with deception or guile to make a belief appear to be knowledge. People expect half-truths in the world of politics, as the government has become a place where many are aware of the misconduct, dishonesty, and corruption often found there. It is the ego's control of so many people that make a half-truth so effective and create the atmosphere where half-truths can thrive.

****

Character assassination is a form of propaganda used by people in power. They can shape people's opinion about someone by continuously promoting falsehoods. These lies will eventually determine how people will feel about a person, a political policy or an agenda. Because of the ego's ability to possess the mind most of the time, what people believe can be slowly eroded away by the ego's gullibility until their conscience selves start to believe these lies are true. Propaganda then becomes a weapon that the powerful can use against the people.

For example, the opposing party started denigrating Hillary Clinton in the early nineties, when she tried to enact a universal healthcare program. She refused to know her place as First Lady and began to include herself in the political process.

She was assaulted with criticisms and lies because she wouldn't kowtow to a passive role, as a First Lady, and instead became an active participant in the political process. For over 25 years, falsehood and fabrication about her were continually repeated. The egos of many people were now beginning to believe that she is a terrible person. Since so many people cannot tell the difference between who they are from their ego, they just know from a 'feeling in their bones' and the deluge of lies about Hillary, that she is some unkind, unpleasant person.

They have now been conditioned to dislike this outstanding, first-class person. There is no reasoning behind the hate; they don't know why, but they just know they don't like her. The reason this happens is because of the ego's gullibility combined with its constant control of the mind and not understanding how the ego operates to influence their belief. Attacking the character of someone with lies is the technique those in authority have used to defeat those who oppose them.

****

Fabrications and half-truths are the technique that detectives use when they question and grill a suspect and tell them how they committed a crime. The obsessive energy drive of the ego can handle this onslaught, but the energy of the rational mind or willpower cannot stand up to this continual badgering coming from detectives. After long enough time, the will can be broken, leaving the ego in charge of the self. The detectives can then easily dupe the ego after hours of interrogation and cause the ego to believe it is guilty of the crime, so the investigators can get an innocent suspect to confess to a crime they never committed because the ego will believe the detectives' accusations.

****

Deception and pretense are how marketing ads, commercials, politicians, people with money, and political ads are used to influence people. Lies or propaganda can be used to control the beliefs of billions of individuals. Because of the lack of knowledge about the ego, people with power are capable of swaying our egos and take advantage of us by influencing our fundamental core beliefs and mislead the masses to achieve their objectives.

****

When we employ awareness, and stay in the now moment, the past can no longer have the terrible influence over our existence. It doesn't matter how abusive, tragic or horrible our life may have been in the past, or how terrible our parents were to us, because with the behavioral tools of awareness, we are armed to overcome and prevail over painful memories or past difficulties.

The ego lives in these memories of the past and will continually return to them because the ego wants you to resolve them. The ego will constantly and obsessively bring up an adverse past event in your mind and create distressing emotions. The ego doesn't enjoy these recollections, but the endeavor does provide the ego with the ability to govern and control the self, and it believes you need to fix these problems from the past.

To take back your authority, you order your ego to 'STOP' recalling memories that are unpleasant. Do this with a silent command in your head to the ego. The ego must give way to your orders, so, you live each moment in the present.

The only things the ego needs to be concerned about are your intentions and dealings with daily situations. The ego has to obey this directive from you and will submit to your authority.

When we let the ego keep reviewing past demoralizing events, we've given away our authority to be the ruler of the self and allowed our ego to be the one in charge of us. We take back our command and control by using the tools of awareness to block the ego's attempts to relive the past. When we regain control of the mind with the skills we've developed, and we live in the present, then a past traumatic event loses its power to affect us.

When we allow the ego to continuously replay a memory from some terrible past event, the demoralizing effect of a past suffering can interfere with our everyday existence. This suffering from post-traumatic stress disorder (PTSD) or some other trauma, can cause a person to lose their desire and enthusiasm for living or even commit suicide.

A more positive outlook on life is needed, along with the behavioral tools that keep you in the present. The ego and the higher self need to let go of negative thoughts and feelings and lighten up. The ego's seriousness can make you an unfriendly and dour person.

To overcome the dire, suffocating control of the ego, you can use exercises that employ various expressions of smiling, as described earlier. Different types of smiles will help to alter the attitude of the ego and the higher self and tell them that you are the one who is in charge! You now can change the influences of the past, because you have the skills to guide you into the present-day life that you have control over.

When you smile, you regain your authority. This simple intentional act tells the ego and the higher self that you are the commander-in-chief who is in charge. The ego and the higher self need to change their view about life. You dictate and command the ego, silently, to 'lighten up,' 'let it be,' and 'enjoy life' because 'it is what it is,' while you practice smiling. This is how you let the ego and higher self know that you're the boss.

Life is something you should enjoy. When you are the ruler of the self, you will discover that life really is a 'bowl of cherries,' that you can enjoy and cherish.

You do not want to continue to be a prisoner, under lock and key of the ego's ability to use terrible past events to hold you captive under its control. You want to live in the present to avoid past miseries. Stay in the now moment to handle life's challenges, and then memories lose their prominence and power.

Suffering wanes with awareness; this requires effort and willpower! The reward is you can reign supreme over the self, and successfully deal with everyday needs and challenges.

****

People suffer from PTSD because of cycles that are repeated by their ego and which operate beneath their conscientiousness. The ego controls them when it plays a loop, repeatedly. Addiction is one of those cycles. Caught in the ego's loop, it will continue to play mind games with them by repeating the same idea, urge, or desire.

Like a needle that's stuck on a spinning phonograph record that repeats the same notes over and over again until you push the needle (the ego) off the track where it's stuck. Due to the ego's influence, each cycle can get stronger until it can be deadly. Unless the circuit or the ego is interrupted, it can lead to an unhappy end.

You get out of the loop with awareness combined with the knowledge that you are the boss of the ego that can tell it what it can do and what it cannot do. When the ego keeps recycling ideas over and over again into your head to get a sugary snack, a cigarette, an alcoholic drink, a pill to alter consciousness, etcetera, you say as forcefully as you can silently, within your mind only, "STOP IT!" and the ego will give up harassing you and leave you in peace. In fact, you can use this behavioral tool anytime the ego repetitively hounds you with thoughts that overwhelm you. This declaration will halt the ego in its tracks so you can regain control of the mind. Addiction begins because of the ego's ability to reside in people's minds so much of the day that it can slowly wear away self-esteem with its critical negativity. Its degrading thoughts cause people to abandon their rational, creative minds to approach life's problems with understanding. So, it's better to fight against the ego's lack of concern for anything but pathos and control, then to allow it to create a pessimistic lethargy about life that needs sugar, tobacco, alcohol, and other drugs to alleviate its tedious, boring life.

The ego has tremendous control of an addict's mind, and with each recurring loop, the ego's desire for immediate satisfaction and a quick fix get stronger and stronger. Many people will relinquish rather than fight against this obsessive force that is the ego. Instead of putting up a struggle to battle against the ego's negative compulsive desires, they yield.

The trouble is that once you hand over control of the self to the ego, you will soon find the ego creates so much conflict, stress, and discontent that they turn to some outside source for help to live a more stimulating life. But this can quickly degenerate into a life of drama that creates worry, anger, and insecurity. Many give up in despair believing there is no way to break out of a recurring cycle, knowing next to nothing about how much power they possess to control their ego and how they would otherwise be able to take control and have command of their lives.

The troubles, overwhelming stresses, and anxieties created by the ego, provoke people to look for some way to escape and seek comfort from some outside source that can dull their senses and make their life more bearable.

What usually provokes the start of these distressing conditions is a lack of understanding that giving the ego the freedom to judge and criticize others allows the ego to turn its censures back on you. The fault-finding by the ego that you allow will undermine your self-confidence and make you insecure, while you relinquish your power to govern and give it to the ego. Instead of allowing the ego to subvert our worthiness, we need the tools of awareness to seize control of our minds and our lives.

The ego is required to obey your demands. You need to realize that this authority is absolutely yours! Your responsibility is to be in charge of the ego and the higher self and take command of the mind.

Until you stand up for your right to be in charge of the ego, the odds of overcoming an addiction will be slim to none. We can succeed and handle life's problems and regain control of our mind and restore the value of ourselves, as well as the value of others, if we have knowledge about the ego, and discover our authority and command over the ego.

****

When someone hurts your feelings, these are the feelings of your sensitive, vulnerable ego, that also affects the higher self. Do not allow yourself to be offended and take it personally! When you feel insulted, and you take it personally, you have empowered this abusive person to have dominion or power over you.

You should realize that this attack is coming from someone else's toddler or ego. Once you discern and consider the source of the assault, you can stand above the fray, and refuse to take it personally. You can sense the emotional hurt and pain and hurt that the ego and the higher self are experiencing; they need comforting, so try to reassure and cheer both up with a smile. Do not allow your ego to take command over you and retaliate. But you can stand up for yourself with good judgement and respond calmly, "What gives you the right to talk to me in that manner?"

When you get heated emotionally and bow to the ego and take umbrage, you've entitled this derogatory person's ego to abandon your behavioral tools of awareness; you've permitted the ego to rule, so you've lost your authority over the self. The offender has taken away your belief in accepting life for what it is. You have conceded your sovereignty as an individual when you take things personally, and that allows the ego to sit on your throne. Your attitude to forgive and just 'let it be' makes you the bigger and more powerful person. Do not take things personally.

Chapter 40

The ego now triumphs over our modern world, because of the use of texting, and Twitter on the iPhone. The chatter, gossip, and prattle with on-screen social communications is a perfect stage for promoting the ego's thoughts, beliefs, and control. Because our young people are living their lives on their smartphones, it has radically changed every aspect of their lives and has altered the nature of their social interactions. The ego has taken over command of our phones and airways among people of every ethnic background, in cities, suburbs, and small towns and among the rich and poor.

The young today are more comfortable today in their bedrooms than interacting with each other. They are not working, they are not managing their money, they are not hanging out with each other any longer like they used to. Instead, they are on their phones, in their room, alone and often distressed.[1]

The ego has them addicted to their phone because they have given in and allowed the ego's obsessively, compulsive desire and drive to keep them apart and independent; it has separated them from the many social interactions they normally would have with each other. We are in a competition to see who can win the battle for our consciousness that's going on between our conscious, rational mind and the ego's limbic brain.

****

The addiction to the smartphones along with a passion for video games has eroded our youth's emotional connections with others. Students are experiencing a loss due to the effect of the phone on learning, because of the interruptions during school, outside of school, and when doing their homework.

They are spending more and more time dwelling on low-quality thinking and content that is mindless and dubious.

****

MIT said the quality of the work being turned in by students has degraded, due to their limited attention span. But this goes far beyond the usual concerns about curtailed attention spans and is showing up in the workplace, as young workers don't want to have face-to-face conversations, but want to text instead. This decrease in our interactions with each other has allowed our rational thinking and creativity to degenerate.

The ego wants this form of communication and loves to live in this bubble with just the two of you. This world that texting and twittering have created, makes you independent and oblivious to other people and the outside world.

When the ego has that much control over you, it's going to make you vulnerable not only to accidents but all the fears, stresses, and insecurities that come about when the ego is in charge.

****

The 'Monitoring the Future' survey, funded by the National Institute on Drug Abuse has asked 12th-graders more than 1,000 questions every year since 1975 and queried eighth through 10th-graders since 1991. The survey asks teens how happy they are and also how much of their leisure time they spend on various activities, including non-screen activities such as in-person social interaction and exercise, and, in recent years, screen activities such as using social media, texting, and browsing the web. The results could not be more explicit: teens who spend more time than average on screen activities are more likely to be unhappy, while those who spend more time than average on non-screen activities are more apt to be happy.[2]

There was not a single exception. Screen activities and unhappiness are linked together. Happiness is more likely to occur when pursuing other interests than on-screen activities. Eighth-graders who spend 10 or more hours a week on social media are 56 percent more likely to say they're unhappy than those who devote less time to social media. Those who spend six to nine hours a week on social media are 47 percent more likely to say they are unhappy than those who use social media less.

A portrait of our young that are emerging from the data is one of a lonely, dislocated generation. Those who visited social-networking sites every day, and saw their friends less frequently, often felt lonely, felt left out, or wished they had more friends, compared to those who had other interests. Teens' feelings of loneliness spiked in 2013 and had remained high since.

Young people who spend three hours a day or more on electronic devices are 35 percent more likely to have a risk factor for suicide, such as making a suicide plan. In 2011, for the first time in 24 years, the teen suicide rate was higher than the teen homicide rate.

****

Personalities are becoming stagnate. You can see couples on their phones when out with others, ignoring their dining experiences, ignoring their kids, ignoring the conversations going on all around them, and communicating with each other via their phones, even though seated directly opposite each other at a table. They continued trying to text each other, after their food was served, with one hand while eating with the other.

The devices we've placed in young people's hands are having profound effects on their lives and making them seriously unhappy. It's not an exaggeration to describe many of today's young millennials are on the brink of the worst mental health crisis in decades, because of the loss of awareness, as the ego becomes the one who rules over them.

****

We have created a perfect world for the ego. It wants to be independent, separate, and apart from others. As a result, people have become more independent and more isolated from each other. The ego has sucked us in and made us addicted to our phones and has possessed our mind, so we no longer have the time to use our rational, creative, problem-solving mind, as we check our phones about one hundred fifty times a day. The ego has us concerned about what we are missing, what we are missing out on, and who we haven't answered back. One of the consequences is the social fabric of our brotherhood that holds us together and makes us human is becoming threadbare. Our social talents, skills, adeptness, abilities, and personalities are dwindling from disuse, as we cooperate less frequently.

Our personality needs to evolve and develop by socially interacting with others. This avoidance and not personally interacting with others are holding back our social development and emotional maturity. These ego-driven activities strengthen the ego's domination and power over us while diminishing our ability to think creatively and logically with reason.

Instead of developing our emotional character, we are degenerating into attitudes that are less caring, with less gratitude for what we have in life and less thankful for the people in our life, as well as losing our spiritual connections with nature and other humans. This detached outlook leads to less face-to-face social interactions, which eventually results in less value on life and increases the potential for violence.

A surge in personal problems causes many to turn to psychiatric medication which exponentially increases the violence. Those involved in mass shooting here in U.S. were on psychotropic drugs, while suicides are occurring at an extremely rapid rate that is many times greater, because of these psych drugs. If people had access to the information about their ego and the behavior tools that can keep it under control, then these problems would go away for these people.

A parent should take away the child's phone and have them read this book before handing their phone back to them.

****

The ego will look to you for protection. If the ego sees you are not fulfilling your responsibilities and not providing protection, then the ego will take up what it feels is its rightful place as the one who should be in control. The ego will take control using anger, blame, avoidance, fear, lying, cheating, evasiveness, feelings of superiority, false bravado, escaping into a fantasy world, etcetera. The ego will take over if you don't assert your command and control of the self by taking control of your mind.

****

The ego has more impact on our lives emotionally, physically, mentally, and psychologically than any other living thing. We have to wonder. Why isn't this precious information about our ego, our engine of energy, not available so people can learn about this vital entity? We find no real intelligent guidance about the ego in the literature except in a philosophical or theoretical sense; or with statements advising us to stay in the present to constrain the ego. But the ego's obsessive desire to be thinking all the time makes it highly unlikely for anyone to remain in the present for any length of time at all unless they are provided with a repertoire of the many behavioral skills needed to maintain that state of 'now.'

It is the ego with its desire to keep us in the dark and its capacity to inflict emotional pain that hinders us from acquiring knowledge about the ego. It will do everything within its power to stop us from gaining information about itself. So, it seems that, the main reason for this ignorance, is a lack of courage among the general population that is the most significant impediment to acquiring knowledge about the ego.

If one were to recommend any literature about how to master the ego, then that person's ego would become so scared, angry, or insecure, there would be no chance that he or she would ever broach any printed matter on that subject. That is the power the ego can have over a person.

The Status social system's lack of acceptance has impaired or damaged self-worth so much that many are unable to take their toddler out shopping for fear of temper tantrums; and many have so little control over their pet dog that its misbehavior interferes with their relationships or hinders their social behavior. So, in the same way, they become afraid of their self and would prefer to operate in the security of ignorance about their self than take a step into gaining knowledge about the ego.

We've become a servant of our ego, under its control. We allow this because we relinquish our oversight and authority unwittingly and timidly. Knowledge about the ego gives us a path to develop the skills to rule the ego and the other selves appropriately and correctly. Without this knowledge, there is no battlefield upon which to fight, because we don't even recognize that there is a battlefield. It is incumbent for us to become the captain who controls the mind and the ego.

****

Marriages and relationships can become adversarial and result in divorce or a breakup. The ego's judgments and critical thoughts can gradually erode a supportive relationship, and the ego's desire for separation and control can lead to divisiveness. Once there is knowledge of the ego's nature, separation becomes less of a problem because the tools of awareness can be used to stop the ego's influence.

Change takes effort. If you want to evolve yourself, you should excel at what you do, but excellence demands hard work. The tools you need have been presented here in these pages to bring the things you desire in life to fruition, so you can become anything you want. It is just a matter of you getting underway or setting out to achieve them.

With the advice provided here, you can thrive and become a confident person who is free of fear, who expresses no anger and who is free of insecurities. You are not, in reality, an emotionally free person until you can have complete command of yourself.

To repeat, if you want to be a success at what you wish, it takes awareness, awareness, awareness; to be a ruler of the self, you need to utilize that awareness with practice, practice, practice.

****

Advice is given to demonstrate how to be proficient at anything you wish. Behavioral skills are offered to help you build relationships, become adept at creating a connection with nature and others, plus show you how to form a stable, intimate alliance.

For a relationship to remain healthy and flourish, the people need to understand the ego and know how to take control of the mind from the ego. You accomplish this by using the tools that promote awareness. You can demand the ego stop being judgmental and critical and require it to look for the many admirable qualities in another to maintain a supportive alliance.

****

If you desire to live an emotional life of joy and bliss, you silently inform the other selves this is how you want to live. But you have to set an example of pretending to be joyful and blissful for them to follow and create those feelings for you. If you want to be more loving, then you need to put a little love in your heart. You tell the 'body' you want the excitement of goosebumps by making the chest area warm, while you relax or soften the muscles around the eyes and create a Mona Lisa type smile as an example for the selves to follow. You can create the kind of social life you desire that can work in tandem with your work.

If you change the human heart, you can change the culture in which you live. You have the power to live the life you want.

The greater propose of this book is to enable you to enhance your character, your rational, creative mind, and your personality to generate a connection with others and create a supportive environment with the knowledge to be a master of your emotional life. Once you have the emotional freedom to be a ruler of the self, you want more than to have satisfaction with your life; you want a life of joy and bliss.

May your life be a blessing. Good luck and Good life.

Bibliography

Part I
Chapter 1

[1] Smythies, J.R. Brain mechanisms and behavior. Academic Press; 1970.

[2] Limbic System: Hippocampus (Section 4, Chapter 5) Neuroscience Online: An Electronic Textbook for the Neurosciences | Department of Neurobiology and Anatomy – The University of Texas Medical School at Houston [Internet]. Nba.uth.tmc.edu. Available from: https://nba.uth.tmc.edu/neuroscience/m/s4/chapter05.html

[3] The Urantia Book. 1995:1176–1229.

Chapter 2

[1] Koch M, Ebert U: Enhancement of the acoustic startle response by stimulation of an excitatory pathway from the central amygdal/basal nucleus of Meynert to the pontine reticular formation. Exp Brain Res 1993; 93:231–241.

[2] Lewis Si, Verberne AJM, Robinson TG, et al: Excitotoxin-induced lesions of the central but not basolateral nucleus of the amygdala modulate the baroreceptor heart rate reflex in conscious rats. Brain Res 1989; 494:232–240.

[3] Clugnet MC, LeDoux JE: Synaptic plasticity in fear conditioning circuits: induction of LIP in the lateral nucleus of the amygdala by stimulation of the medial geniculate body. J Neurosci 1990; 10:2818–2824.

[4] Tranel D, Hyman BT: Neuropsychological correlates of bilateral amygdala damage. Arch Neurol 1990; 47:349–355.

[5] Lorenzini CA, Bucherelli C, Ciachetti LM, et al: Effects of nucleus basolateralis amygdalae neurotoxic lesions on aversive conditioning in the rat. Physiol Behav 1991; 49:765–770.

[6] Maren S, Aharonov C, Fanselow MS: Retrograde abolition of conditioned fear after excitotoxic lesions in the basolateral amygdala of rats. Behav Neurosci 1996; 110:718–726.

[7] Helmstetter FJ, Bellgowan PS: Effects of muscimol applied to the basolateral amygdala on acquisition and expression of contextual fear conditioning in rats. Behav Neurosci 1994; 108:1005–1009.

[8] Sanders SK, Shekhar A: Blockade of GABAA receptors in the region of the anterior basolateral amygdala of rats elicits increases in heart rate and blood pressure. Brain Res 1991; 576: 101–110.

[9] Davis M: The role of the amygdala in fear and anxiety. Annu Rev Neurosci 1992; 15:353–375.

[10] Graeff FG, Silveira MCL, Nogueira RL, et al: Role of the amygdala and periaqueductal gray in anxiety and panic. Behav Brain Res 1993; 58:123–131.

[11] Davis M. The role of the amygdala in conditioned fear, in The Amygdala: Neurobiological Aspects of Emotion, Memory and Mental Dysfunction, edited by Aggleton J. New York, Wiley. 1992; 255–305.

[12] LeDoux JE, Iwata J, Cicchetti P, et al: Different projections of the central amygdaloid nucleus mediate autonomic and behavioral correlates of conditioned fear. J Neurosci 1988; 8:2517–2529.

[13] Adolphs R, Tranel D, Damasio H, et al: Fear and the human amygdala. J Neurosci 1995; 15:5879–5891.

[14] Homeostatic regulation of sleep: A role for preoptic area neurons. Gvilia I, Xu F, McGinty D, Szymusiak R.J Neurosci. 2006 Sept. 13; 26(37):9426–33.

[15] Sleep-promoting functions of the hypo-thalamic median preoptic nucleus: inhibition of arousal systems. McGinty D, Gong H, Suntsova N, Alam, Methippara M, Guzman-Marin R. Arch Ital Bio. 2004 Jul;142(4):501–9.

[16] Preoptic area sleep-regulating mechanisms. Szymusiak R, Steininger T, Alam N, McGinty D. Arch Ital Biol. 2001 Feb; 139(1–2):77–92.

Chapter 3

[1] Bliss TV, Collingridge GL. A synaptic model of memory: long-term potentiation in the hippocampus. Nature 361. 1993 Jan; (6407):31–9.

[2] Stein PSG. Neurons, Networks, and Motor Behavior. MIT Press. 1999; 38–44.

[3] Grünewald R.A., Yoneda Y., Shipman J.M., Sagar H.J. Idiopathic focal dystonia: a disorder of muscle spindle afferent processing. Brain. 1997; 120:2179–2185.

[4] Dafny, N. and Feldman, S. Effects of caudate nucleus stimulation. Electroencephalog. Clin.Neurophysiol. 1967; 23:546–557.

[5] Dafny, N. and Feldman, S. Responsiveness of posterior hypothalamic neurons to striatal & peripheral stimuli. Exp. Neurol. 1968; 21:397–412.

[6] Feldman, S. and Dafny, N. Modification of single cell responses in the posterior hypothalamus to sensory stimuli by caudate and globus pallidus stimulation. Brain Res. 1968; 10:402–417.

Chapter 5

[1] Maslow, A. H & Honigmann, J.J. Synergy: Some notes of Ruth Benedict. American Anthropologist. 1970; 72(1):320–33.

[2] Royal Society Open Science. 2017 Sept. 20.

Chapter 6

[1] Elkins, Rueckert, and McCarty. The Law of One; 1984.

[2] Masaru Emoto. Messages from Water. 1999; 1(2):89–92.

[3] Masaru Emoto. Messages from Water. 2001; 2(7):103–106.

[4] Knobloch H, Gesell AL, Amatruda CS, Pasamanick B. Gesell and Amatruda's developmental diagnosis: The evaluation and management of normal and abnormal neuropsychologic development in infancy and early childhood. Harper & Row; 1974.

[5] Wood, A. M., Joseph, S., & Maltby, J. PersonalPages.Manchester.ac.uk, Gratitude uniquely predicts satisfaction with life: Incremental validity above the domains and facets of the Five Factor Model. Personality and Individual Differences. 2008; 45:49–54.

[6] Gervais, M. & Wilson, D. The evolution and functions of laughter and humor: A synthetic approach. The Quarterly Review of Biology. 2005; 80(4):395–430.

Chapter 7

[1] Richards K, Campenni C, Muse-Burke J. Self-care, and well-being in mental health professionals: The mediating effects of self-awareness and mindfulness. Journal of Mental Health Counseling. 2010 Jul 1; 32(3):247-64.

[2] Staikova E, Gomes H, Tartter V, McCabe A, Halperin JM. Pragmatic deficits and social impairment in children with ADHD. Journal of Child Psychology and Psychiatry. 2013 Dec;54(12):1275-83.

Chapter 10

[1] The Urantia Book. 1995; 1229–1240.

[2] Wood, A. M., Joseph, S., & Maltby, J. PersonalPages.Manchester.ac.uk, Gratitude uniquely predicts satisfaction with life: Incremental validity above the domains and facets of the Five Factor Model. Personality and Individual Differences. 2008; 45:49–54.

Chapter 11

[1] Laffey JG, Kavanagh BP. Carbon dioxide and the critically ill – too little of a good thing? Lancet. 1999; 354(9186):1283–1286.

[2] Jennifer and Russell Stark: authors of the book The Carbon Dioxide Syndrome; 2009.

[3] Laffey JG, Kavanagh BP. Carbon dioxide and the critically ill – too little of a good thing? Lancet. 1999; 354(9186):1283–1286.

[4] Jennifer and Russell Stark: authors of the book The Carbon Dioxide Syndrome, 2009.

Part II
Chapter 12

[1] Christian Bohr. Wikipedia; 1904.

[2] Bohr C, Hasselbalch K, Krogh A. Concerning a biologically important relationship–the influence of the carbon dioxide content of blood on its oxygen binding. Skand. Arch. Physiol. 1904; 16:402–12.

[3] Irzhak, L. I. Christian Bohr (On the Occasion of the 150th Anniversary of His Birth). Human Physiology. 2005; 31(3): 366–368.

[4] Ventral Striatum. sciencedirect.com Available from:
http://www.sciencedirect.com/topics/neuroscience/ventral-striatum

Chapter 13

[1] Pribram, K.H. Languages of The Brain. Prentice-Hall. 1971; 28–43.

[2] Vanderloos, H. Improperly oriented cells in the cortex and its bearing on growth and cell proliferation. Bulletin of Johns Hospital. 1965; 117:228–250.

[3] Pinto S., Roseberry A. G., Liu H., Diano S., Shanabrough M., Cai X., et al. Rapid rewiring of arcuate nucleus feeding circuits by leptin. Science 304. 2004; 110–11510.

[4] Gellhorn. & Loofbourrow. Emotional Disorders. Harper & Row, 1963.

[5] R. Szymusiak. Thermoregulation during Sleep and Sleep Deprivation. Encyclopedia of Neuroscience. 2009; 971–975.

[6] Herrick, C.J. The functions of the olfactory parts of the cerebral cortex. Proc. Nat. Acad. Sci. 1933; 19:7–14.

[7] Zald DH, Pardo JV. Emotion, olfaction, and the human amygdala: amygdala activation during aversive olfactory stimulation. Proceedings of the National Academy of Sciences. 1997 Apr 15; 94(8):4119–24.

[8] Price J. L., Slotnick B. M., Revial M. F. Olfactory projections to the hypothalamus. J. Comp. Neurol. 1991; 306:447–461.

[9] Ventrolateral preoptic nucleus. wikipedia.com. Available from: https://en.wikipedia.org/wiki/Ventrolateral_preoptic_nucleus

[10] Nauta, W.J.H. Hypothalantic regulation of sleep in rats: an experimental study. Journal Neurophysiol. 1946; 9:285–316.

[11] Sallanon, M. et al. Long-lasting insomnia induced by preoptic neuron lesions and its transient reversal by muscimol injection into the posterior hypothalamus in the cat. Neuroscience 32. 1989; 669–683.

[12] Chou TC, Scammell TE, Gooley JJ, Gaus SE, Saper CB, Lu J. Critical role of dorsomedial hypothalamic nucleus in a wide range of behavioral circadian rhythms. J Neurosci. 2003; 23:10691–10702.

[13] John J, Kumar VM. Effect of NMDA lesion of the medial preoptic neurons on sleep and other functions. Sleep. 1998; 21:587–598.

[14] Gvilia I, Xu F, McGinty D, Szymusiak R. Homeostatic regulation of sleep: a role for preoptic area neurons. J Neurosci. 2006; 26:9426–9433.

[15] Lu J, Greco , Shiromani P, Saper CB. Effect of lesions of the ventrolateral preoptic nucleus on NREM and REM sleep. J Neurosci. 2000; 20:3830–3842.

[16] Morairty S, Rainnie D, McCarley R, Greene R. Disinhibition of ventrolateral preoptic area sleep-active neurons by adenosine: a new mechanism for sleep promotion. Neuroscience. 2004; 123:451–457.

[17] P.M. Fuller, J. Lu. Encyclopedia of Neuroscience. 2009; 929–936.

[18] Kalra et al. Interacting Appetite-Regulating Pathways in the Hypothalamic Regulation of Body Weight. Endocrine Reviews. 20(1): 68–100.

Chapter 15

[1] Olds, M.E. and Olds, J. Approach-avoidance analysis of rat diencephalon. Journal Comp. Neurol. 1963; 120:259–295.

[2] Wurtz, R.H. and Olds, J. Amygdaloid stimulation and operant reinforcement in the rat. Journal Comp. Physiol. Psychol. 1963; 56:941–949.

[3] Wagner, A. R., Thomas, E., & Norton, T. Conditioning with electrical stimulation of motor cortex: Evidence of a possible source of motivation. Journal of Comparative and Physiological Psychology. 1967; 64(2):191–199.

[4] Olds, J. Differential effects of drive and drugs on self-stimulation at brain sites. In Electrical Stimulation of the Brain. D.E. Sheer (ED) Austin: Univ. of Texas Press; 1961.

Chapter 16

[1] Gesell, A.L. and llg, F.L. Child and development: an introduction to the study of human growth. Harper and Brothers; 1949.

[2] 2 Hayward, J.N. and Smith, W.K. Influence of limbic system on neurohypophysis. Arch. Neurol. 1963; 9:171–177.

[3] Knobloch, H. and Pasamanick, B. Gesell and Amatruda's Developmental Diagnosis. Harper and Row; 1974.

[4] Schwartzbaum, J.S. Discrimination behavior after amygdalectomy in monkeys. Journal of Comparative and Physiological Psychology. 1965; 60:314–319.

[5] Marta Isabel Garrido, et al, Surprise responses in the human brain demonstrate statistical learning under high concurrent cognitive demand; NPJ Science of Learning. 2016; 1(16006).

[6] Schaffer, H.R. and Emerson, P.E. The development of social attachments in infancy. Monographs of the Society for Research in Child Development. 1964; 94:29.

[7] Bowlby, J. Separation anxiety. Int. journal PSA. 1960; 41:89–113.

[8] Arnold, M.B. Brain function in emotion. In P. Black (Ed.) Physiological Correlates of Emotion. Academic Press; 1970.

Chapter 17

[1] Smythies, J.R. Brain mechanisms and behavior. Academic Press; 1970.

[2] Lesse, H. Rhinencephalic eletrophysiological activity during emotional behavior in cats. In L.J. West and M. Greenblatt (Eds.), Explorations in the physiology of Emotions. A.P.A. Psychiat. Res. Reports. 1960; 12:224.

[3] Endroczi, E. Lissak, K. and Kovacs, S. The inhibitory influence of archicortical structures on pituitary-adrenal function. Acta Physiol. Acad. Sci. Hung. 1959; 16:17–22.

[4] Kawakami, M., Seto, K., Tevasawa, E. and Yoshida, K. Mechanisms in the limbic system controlling reproductive functions of the ovary with special reference to the positive feedback of progestin to the hippocampus. Progressive Brain Res. 1967; 27:69–102.

[5] Knigge, K.M. Adrenocbrtical Response to stress in rats with lesions in hippocampus and amygdala. Proceedings of the Society for Experimental Biology and Medicine. 1961; 108:18–21.

[6] Ursin, H. and Kaada, B.R. Functional localization within the amygdaloid complex in the cat. EEG Clin. Neurophysiol. 1969; 12:1–20.

[7] Sokolov, E.N. Higher nervous functions: the orienting reflex. Annual Review of Physiology. Stanford, Calif.: Annual Reviews. 1963; 544–580.

[8] Schwartzbaum,J.S. Changes in reinforcing properties of stimuli following ablation of the amygdaloid complex in monkey. Journal of Comparative and Physiological Psychology. 1960; 53:388–395.

[9] Schwartzbaum, J.S. Discrimination behavior after amygdalectomy in monkeys. Journal of Comparative and Physiological Psychology. 1965; 60:314–319.

[11] Schaffer, H.R. and Emerson, P.E. The development of social attachments in infancy. Monographs of the Society for Research in Child Development. 1964; 94:29.

[12] Olds, M.E. and Olds, J. Approach-avoidance analysis of rat diencephalon. Journal Comp. Neurol. 1963; 120:259–295.

[13] Yarrow, L.J. Separation from parents during childhood. Review of Child Development research, Vol. 1. Russell Sage Foundation; 1954.

[14] Stevens, J.R., Glaser, G.H. and Maclean, P.D. The influence of sodium amytal on the recollection of seizure states. Tran. Amer. Neurol. Assoc. 1954; 79(1):40–95.

[15] Ursin, H. and Kaada, B.R. Functional localization within the amygdaloid complex in the cat. EEG Clin. Neurophysiol. 1969; 12:1–20.

[16] Ursin, H. and Kaada, B.R. Subcortical structures mediating attention response induced by amygdala stimulation. Exp. Neurol. 1960; 2:109–122.

[17] Andersen, R. Differences in the course of learning as measured by various memory tasks after amygdalectomy. In E. Fitchcock, L. Laitinen and K. Vaemet (Eds.). Psychosurgery. Springfield, Ill.:Charles C. Thomas. 1972; 177–183.

Chapter 18

[1] Gesell, A.L. and llg, F.L. Child and development: an introduction to the study of human growth. Harper and Brothers; 1949.

Chapter 19

[1] Dafny, N. and Feldman, S. Effects of caudate nucleus stimulation. Electroencephalog. Clin. Neurophysiol. 1967; 23:546–557.

[2] Dafny, N. and Feldman, S. Responsiveness of posterior hypothelan-tic neurons to striatal and peripheral stimuli. Exp. Neurol. 1968; 21:397–412.

[3] Feldman, S. and Dafny, N. Modification of single cell responses in the posterior hypothalamus to sensory stimuli by caudate and globus pallidus stimulation. Brain Res. 1968; 10:402–417.

[4] Buchwald, N.A., Wuyers, E.J., Okuma, T. and Heuser, G. The caudate spindle. 1: Electrophysiological Properties. EEG Clin. Neurophysiol. 1961; 13:509–518.

Chapter 20

[1] Gesell, A.L. and llg, F.L. Child and development: an introduction to the study of human growth. Harper and Brothers; 1949.

Chapter 21

[1] Gesell, A.L. and Ilg, F.L. Child and development: an introduction to the study of human growth. Harper and Brothers; 1949.

[2] Arnold, M.B. Brain function in emotion. In P. Black (Ed.)Physiological Correlates of Emotion. Academic Press; 1970.

[3] Wurtz, R.H. and Olds, J. Amygdaloid stimulation and operant reinforcement in the rat. Journal Comp. Physiol. Psychol. 1963; 56:941–949.

[4] Smythies, J.R. Brain mechanisms and behavior. Academic Press; 1970.

[5] Maclean, P.D. and Ploug, D.W. Cerebral representation of penile erection. Journal Neurophysiol. 1962; 25:30–55.

Chapter 22

[1] Piaget, J. The Construction of Reality in the Child. Trans. by M. Cook. N.Y. Basic Books; 1954.

[2] Gesell, A.L. and Ilg, F.L. Child and development: an introduction to the study of human growth. Harper and Brothers; 1949.

Chapter 23

[1] Lindsley, D.B. The role of nonspecific reticulo-thalamocortical systems in emotion. In P. Black (Ed.) Physiological Correlates of Emotion. Academic Press; 1970.

Chapter 24

[1] Gesell, A.L. and Ilg, F.L. Child and development: an introduction to the study of human growth. Harper and Brothers; 1949.

Chapter 25

[1] Orbach, J., Milner, B. and Rasmussen, T. Learning and retention in monkeys after amygdala hippocampal resection. Arch. Neurol. 1960; 3:230–251.

[2] Andersen, P., Eccles, J. C. and Lyning, Y. Feedback inhibition via basket cells in the hippocampus. Journal Neurophysiol., 1964; 27:592–608.

[3] Simpson, D.A. The efferent fibers of the hippocampus in the monkey. Journal Neurol. Neurosurg. Psychiat. 1952; 15:79.

Chapter 26

[1] Sokolov, E.N. Higher nervous functions: The Orienting Reflex. Annual Review of Physiology; Stanford, Calif. 1963; 545–580.

[2] Gesell, A.L. and llg, F.L. Child and development: an introduction to the study of human growth. Harper and Brothers; 1949.

Chapter 27

[1] Satoshi Terada; Oscillatory interaction between amygdala and hippocampus coordinates behavioral modulation based on reward expectation. Front Behav Neurosci. 2013; 7:177.

[2] Sokolov, E.N. Higher nervous functions: the orienting reflex. Annual Review of Physiology. Stanford, Calif.: Annual Reviews. 1963; 544–580.

[3] Bruner, J.S. On perceptual readiness. Psychological Review. 1957; 64:123–152.

[4] Maccoby, E.E. Selective auditory attention in children. In L.P. Lipsitt and C.C. Spiker (Eds.) Advances in Child Dev. and Behavior. Vol. III N.Y.: Academic Press; 1967.

[5] Grossman, S.P. A textbook of Physiological Psychology. JohnWiley and Sons; 1967.

[6] Jasper, H.H., Proctor, L.D., Knighton, R.S., Noshay, W.C. and Costello, R.T. (Eds.) The Reticular Formation of the Brain. Boston: Little Brown; 1958.

[7] Livingston,R.B. Central control of receptors and sensory transmission sys. In Handbook of Phys. Vol. I., J. Gield. (Eds.) Baltimore: Williams and Wilkins; 1959.

Chapter 28

[1] Knobloch, H. and Pasamanick, B. Gesell and Amatruda's Developmental Diagnosis. Harper and Row; 1974.

[2] Fraiberg, S. On the sleep disturbances of early childhood. The Psychoanalytic Study Of The Child. International Universities Press. 1950; 285–309.

[3] Gesell, A.L. and llg, F.L. Child and development: an introduction to the study of human growth. Harper and Brothers; 1949.

Chapter 29

[1] Fraiberg, S. On the sleep disturbances of early childhood. The Psychoanalytic Study of The Child. International Universities Press. 1950; 285–309.

1 Gesell, A.L. and llg, F.L. Child and development: an introduction to the study of human growth. Harper and Brothers; 1949.

Chapter 30

[1] Gesell, A.L. and llg, F.L. Child and development: an introduction to the study of human growth. Harper and Brothers; 1949.

Chapter 31

[1] Maclean, P.D. The hypothalamus and emotional behavior. In W. Haymaker, E. Anderson & W. Nauta (Ed.) The Hypothalamus. 1969; 659–679.

[2] Dafny, N. and Feldman, S. Effects of caudate nucleus stimulation. Electroencephalog. Clin. Neurophysiol. 1967; 23: 546–557.

[3] Dafny, N. and Feldman, S. Responsiveness of posterior hypothelan-tic neurons to striatal and peripheral stimuli. Exp. Neurol. 1968; 21:397–412.

[4] Feldman, S. and Dafny, N. Modification of single cell responses in the posterior hypothalamus to sensory stimuli by caudate and globus pallidus stimulation. Brain Res. 1968; 10:402–417.

[5] Eccles, J.C. The Understanding of the Brain. McGraw Hill; 1973.

Chapter 32

[1] Gesell, A.L. and Ilg, F.L. Child and development: an introduction to the study of human growth. Harper and Brothers; 1949.

Chapter 33

[1] Nauta, W. and Haymaker, W. Hypothalantic nuclei and fiber connections. In the hypothalamus. W. Haymaker, E. Anderson, and W. Nauta (Ed.), Thomas Books. 1969; 136–209.

[2] Simpson, D.A. The efferent fibers of the hippocampus in the monkey. Journal Neurol. Neurosurg. Psychiat. 1952; 15:79.

[3] Andersen, P., Eccles, J. C. and Lyning, Y. Feedback inhibition via basket cells in the hippocampus. Journal Neurophysiol. 1964; 27:592–608.

[4] Endroczi, E. Lissak, K. and Kovacs, S. The inhibitory influence of archicortical structures on pituitary-adrenal function. Acta Physiol. Acad. Sci. Hung., 1959; 16:17–22.

[5] Kawakami, M., Seto, K., Tevasawa, E. and Yoshida, K. Mechanisms in the limbic system controlling reproductive functions of the ovary with special reference to the positive feedback of progestin to the hippocampus. Progressive Brain Res. 1967; 27:69–102.

[6] Knigge, K.M. Adrenocbrtical Response to stress in rats with lesions in hippocampus and amygdala. Proceedings of the Society for Experimental Biology and Medicine. 1961; 108:18–21. 28.

[7] Kawakami, M., Seto, K., Tevasawa, E. and Yoshida, K. Mechanisms in the limbic system controlling reproductive functions of the ovary with special reference to the positive feedback of progestin to the hippocampus. Progressive Brain Res. 1967; 27:69–102.

[8] Andersen, P., Eccles, J. C. and Lyning, Y. Feedback inhibition via basket cells in the hippocampus. Journal Neurophysiol. 1964; 27:592–608.

[9] Eccles, J.C. The Understanding of the Brain. McGraw Hill, 1973.

[10] Pickenhain, L. and Klingberg, F. Hippocampal slow wave activity as a correlate of basic behavioral mechanisms in the rat. Progressive Brain Res. 1967; 27:218–227.

[11] Rothfield, & Harman. The relation of the hippo-campal-fomix system to the control of rage re-sponses in cats. Journal Comp. Neurol. 1954; 101:265–282.

[12] Olds, M.E. and Olds, J. Approach-avoidance analysis of rat diencephalon. Journal Comp. Neurol. 1963; 120:259–295.

[13] Ullmann, L.P. and Krasner, L.A. Psychological Approach To Abnormal Behavior. Prentice-Hall; 1969.

[14] Meissner, W.W. Learning and memory in the Korsakoff Syndrome. International journal of Neuropsychiatry. 1968; 4(1):6–20.

Chapter 34

[1] Gesell, A.L. and llg, F.L. Child and development: an introduction to the study of human growth. Harper and Brothers; 1949.

Chapter 35

[1] Smythies, J.R. Brain mechanisms and behavior. Academic Press; 1970.

[2] Grossman, S.P. A textbook of Physiological Psychology. JohnWiley and Sons; 1967.

[3] Nauta, W. and Haymaker, W. Hypothalantic nuclei and fiber connections. In the hypothalamus. W. Haymaker, E. Anderson, and W. Nauta (Ed.), Thomas Books. 1969; 136–209.

Chapter 36

[1] Bailey, P., von Bonin, G.; The Isocortex of Man. Urbana, Ill., Univ. of Illinois Press; 1951.

[2] Lorente de N. R., Cerebral Cortex. Chapter XV in J. F. Fulton: Physiology of the Nervous System, London, New York, Toronto, Oxford Univ. Press.

[3] Netter, F. H. The CIBA Collection of Medical Illustrations, Section III, Cerebral Cortex – Structure, Plate 48. 73

Chapter 38

[1] Chevalier G., Sinatra ST., Oschman J., et al. Earthing (grounding) the human body reduces blood viscosity: a major factor in cardiovascular disease. Journal of Alternative and Complementary Medicine. 2013; 19(2):102–110.

[2] Ober C., Sinatra S., Zucker M. Earthing: The Most Important health Discovery ever! 2014; 124–128.

[3] Journal of Alternative and Complementary Medicine. 2013 Feb; 19(2):102–10.

[4] Chevalier, G. The effect of grounding the human body on mood. Psychological Reports. 2015; 116(2):534–42.

[5] Chamberlin K, Smith W, Chirgwin C, Appasani S, Rioux P. Analysis of the charge exchange between the human body and ground: evaluation of "earthing" from an electrical perspective. Journal of chiropractic medicine. 2014 Dec 1;13(4):239–46.

[6] G. Chevalier et.al. Earthing: Health Implications of Reconneccting the Human body to the Earth's Surface Electrons. Journal of Environmental and Public Health; 2012.

[7] Sperry, R.W. Hemisphere deconnection and unity of conscious awareness. American Psychologist. 1968; 23:723–733.

[8] Sperry, R.W. Perception in the absence of the neocortical commissures. Perception and Its Disorders, Res. Publ. 1970; 48.

[9] de Lacoste-Utamsing, C.; Holloway, R. L., Sexual dimorphism in the human corpus caflosum. Science. 1982; 216:1431–1432.

[10] Ho, K.; Roessmann, U.; Straumfjord, J. V.; Monroe, G., Analysis of brain weight I. Adult brain weight in relation to sex, race, and age. Arch. PathoL Lab. Med. 1980; 104:635–639.

Chapter 40

[1] Jill Filipovie. The Feminist H-spot pursuit of Happiness. 2017 May.

[2] Monitoring the Future: A Continuing Study of American Youth (8th- and 10th-Grade Surveys) (12th-Grade Survey), 2014. 2015; 10–26.

CPSIA information can be obtained
at www.ICGtesting.com
Printed in the USA
BVHW040305090321
602011BV00005B/457